DISCLAIMER

This book is designed to give readers some useful tips and ideas. It does not replace expert advice from medical or behavioral specialists. It is recommended that you seek advice from qualified professionals if you are concerned in any way.

CLUTTER-FREE FOREVER

Embrace Minimalism, Declutter Your Life and Never Iron
Again

-A *Nourish Your Soul* Book-

Julie Schooler

This book is dedicated to my Dad, Ian, who owns just four pairs of shoes.
And he only has that many because he had to buy a special pair when he took up lawn bowls.

CONTENTS

READER GIFT: THE HAPPY20

There is no doubt that decluttering improves your life, but you
can choose to be happy any time.
To remind you to squeeze the best out every single
day, I created:

THE HAPPY20
20 Free Ways to Boost Happiness in 20 Seconds or Less

A PDF gift for you with quick ideas to improve your mood and
add a little sparkle to your day.

Head to **JulieSchooler.com/gift** to grab your copy today.

1

FINDING SPACE TO BREATHE

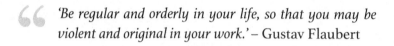
'Be regular and orderly in your life, so that you may be violent and original in your work.' – Gustav Flaubert

CLUTTER TROUBLE

- Is your home filled with stuff?
- Want to declutter but not sure how?
- Are you longing for some space in your hectic life?

As a busy, modern mama, you know there must be more to life than stuffing clothes back into too-full closets, finding ways to cook dinner around mountains of mess on kitchen counters and stumbling on toys left all over the floor.

You have heard about decluttering and know it could be an answer to your woes. Maybe you have even read about it and given it a go. After all, the end result sounds so inviting—easily finding something to wear, having a smooth, clear surface to chop vegetables on and avoiding the agony of stepping on a piece of LEGO!

But some of the instructions sound far-fetched, abstract or just too hard.

You need easy, practical tips to help you declutter in a realistic way that addresses the fact that you have lots of demands on your time, other people in your home to think about and that you don't want to become an extreme minimalist with only one towel to your name.

Even busy mamas like you can embrace minimalism in the best way that suits you and your family. In fact, decluttering can be easier, less time consuming and more fun than you think.

You really want to declutter.

The trouble is, you don't know how to start.

DECLUTTER AND THRIVE

In less than a couple of hours, this book suggests practical ways to declutter your home and your life. There are no hard and fast methods of how to declutter the 'right way'. Instead, this guide offers an adaptable game plan specially designed for the busy mama to make decluttering as easy as possible.

Not only will this book show you how to start decluttering, but it will give you guidance on how to keep up the momentum and finish it completely without it taking eternity.

It answers all your burning questions such as what minimalism is and how it applies to you, how to deal with the emotions evoked by sentimental items and what to do if your screwdriver, bra or tax returns don't spark joy but you feel like you have to keep them anyway!

In addition to decluttering guidance, this book provides ways to organize your remaining things and helps you find the best ways to get rid of items you no longer want so they don't end up in a landfill, but instead in a new home with someone who loves and uses them.

In the final few chapters, this book cuts through the confusion around changing your consumer behavior so you can keep your house in order, provides compelling reasons why minimalism is for everyone and explains how decluttering your home can lead to life improvements beyond your wildest dreams.

You may not believe it now, but you will move from just coping to thriving.

MAMA ON A MISSION

I am not a Japanese tidying expert. I am simply a wife, a mama of two young kids and a typical suburban home owner with a house full of stuff. And I was sick of not living my best life due to dealing with trivial things. I was sick of feeling like there was no space to breathe. I was sick of being overwhelmed and irritated all the time.

I didn't want to nag the kids to put away their toys every single night. I didn't want to feel resentful about being late because we couldn't find a shoe. There had to be a better way to live. Just because everyone has the same problems doesn't make it right.

So, I did what I always do. I read. A lot. I read dozens of books and articles and searched all over the Internet. I also spent a month decluttering my own home and posting about it every day.

I have distilled the avalanche of advice and my learnings from a month of decluttering into simple and practical tips to help busy, modern mamas, just like you and me, to embrace minimalism in a realistic way plus declutter our homes and our lives once and for all.

Surprisingly, even though I read widely, I couldn't find a clear, gimmick-free guide like this one.

Again, I wrote the book I wanted to read.

BENEFITS OF DECLUTTERING

Think how great it will be when you declutter your home and your life. There are benefits in so many areas:

- A tidier house that is a breeze to keep clean
- Finding everything you love and use easily in your organized home
- More time to spend with your family on fun experiences and activities
- Fewer arguments over toys, plus kids who create, imagine and dream
- Knowing your unwanted stuff is being used by people who need and love it
- Never being stuck in a consumer culture in which you buy stuff to feel good
- Living your best life with the time and space to do exactly what you want to do
- And, of course, jettisoning all those crumpled shirts and never ironing again!

RECOMMENDED BY MAMAS FOR MAMAS

Busy mamas are happy to recommend this one short, easy-to-read guide. They are excited that minimalism doesn't have to mean going without and that decluttering can be fun and easy. The tips on how to overcome the emotional aspects of decluttering were a big help. Modern mamas are relieved at the many great alternatives to the landfill for all their unwanted items. How to extend minimalism into other areas of their lives was an unexpected yet valuable bonus.

This refreshingly non-judgmental book includes tips on:

- Deciding what to do with unwanted items: donate, sell, give away or trash
- Reducing your consumption going forward by hiring or not purchasing at all
- Embracing minimalism in other areas of your life including a digital declutter
- Making decisions about kids' artwork, old photo albums and that unsightly vase left to you by your dearly departed grandmother

BEST GIFT OF ALL

My promise is that if you follow the suggestions in this book, your house will feel spacious, you will feel better, life will be relaxed once again, and you will give the world the best gift of all —a mama who is calm and happy.

When you declutter your life, you become a lighthouse for those around you. You won't have to say anything directly. They will notice that you seem lighter. They will detect that you have more time and energy. They will mention how in control you look.

They will want to know the secret to your serene state.

. . .

Take Back the Space

Having lots of stuff crammed into your space is a cruel and unnecessary way to live.

Don't wait another restless night in your overcrowded bedroom to read this book.

Be the modern minimalist mama you want to be—not when the 'time is right', but today.

Find the real you—the one that you know is in there but has been drowned by all your stuff.

Read this book, take action and gain your life back.

Help is at Hand

Think of reading this book as the start of your new life—one based on focusing primarily on the important things. A life in which everything you need and love is retained and nothing more. A life that, at its heart, is designed to create security, joy, meaning and freedom.

And know that taking action will help you and your family, now and for the rest of your time on this one planet we all call home.

2

WHY DO WE ALL WANT TO DECLUTTER?

 'Happiness is not having what you want. It is wanting what you have.' – Rabbi Hyman Schachtel

THE FAVORITE BOWL

"Don't use that bowl. It's my favorite one—it is very special to me." I made an attempt to take a bowl from my seven-year-old, Dylan, who was trying to tip what looked like the whole contents of the cereal box into it.

The bowl is, as far as I know, one of a kind. It is small and white with tiny pictures that represent different nursery rhymes on the inside edges. There is an image of Mary's little lamb and another of Humpty Dumpty. It was specially bought for me when I was small by my beloved late grandmother to use when I visited her. Over the years, I had somehow squirreled it into my possession. It probably isn't worth any money, but it has extremely high sentimental value.

Yes, it is in the drawer with the other bowls as I don't want it boxed up, but I had tucked it underneath so it could only be unearthed if every other dish was in use. Somehow, Dylan had found it.

Dylan looked up at me, a puzzled frown creasing his normally smooth features. "But, Mama, if it means so much to you, why don't we use it more?" Although I would hate to see it broken, the child's logic made perfect sense. My grandmother would have appreciated that I still had the bowl. She would have relished the fact that I loved it so much. And she would be especially delighted that her great-grandson was now using it.

This innocent question over breakfast led me to a one-month project to declutter my house and ultimately to write this book.

What's the Problem?

Decluttering is a major topic of interest these days, but why? What about it has hit a nerve with people? How come the response is so animated when someone posts an image of their tidy closet online? Why is it now okay to admit to your friends that you may have a hoarding problem? (A close friend said recently, "not everywhere, just with shoes.") Why does it seem that everyone wants to declutter?

Sure, the latest phenomenon can be traced to *The Life-Changing Magic of Tidying Up*, the 2014 book by Japanese tidying expert, Marie Kondo. It became a best seller and stayed number one on the charts for months. Although its popularity diminished slightly after a couple of years, the Netflix documentary, *Tidying Up with Marie Kondo*, released in early 2019, reignited the still smoldering interest in decluttering.

But why was it a best seller in the first place?

The need for decluttering is at an all-time high:

- Over 25% of people in the U.S. can't park their cars in the garage due to it being filled with other items.
- *Psychology Today* reported that messy homes leave us feeling anxious, helpless and overwhelmed.
- The U.S.A. has 3% of the world's children and 40% of the world's toys.
- Studies have shown a link between higher stress in women home owners and the more stuff they have.
- More than ten percent of households in the U.S. pay for offsite storage.
- On average, homes in the U.S. contain more TVs than people.
- Using MRI scanning, research has found clutter has a negative effect on our brain's ability to concentrate and process information.

Nowadays, our lives are full to the brim, not just with stuff, but with tight schedules, crowded inboxes, a myriad of structured kid's activities and notifications blaring inane information at us every minute. It is way too much for our prehistoric brains to deal with.

We long for the endless summer days of our childhoods—riding bikes, swimming and basking in the afternoon sun. We remember as young adults being able to pack a bag and go on a road trip with not much more than our wallets and a toothbrush. And with rose-tinted nostalgia we think about the time before mobile phones when dinner wasn't rushed and weekend lie-ins were the norm.

Then someone comes along and says all we have to do is get rid of our stuff and this magical life of freedom will drop into our laps. Well, Marie Kondo hasn't said that directly, but the promise of it is palpable in her work.

Can it be that simple? Well, yes and no. Decluttering will help you find yourself and what is important to you again under all your stuff. But it takes work, some dedication and decision-making to create and keep up this feeling of freedom. You wouldn't be reading this book if you weren't willing to give it a go.

Can't you almost taste it?

Definitions

Before we go any further, let's get some definitions out of the way and then you can decide if decluttering really is for you right now.

Clutter – a lot of things in an untidy state, especially things that are not useful or necessary (Collins dictionary)

Decluttering – removing things you do not need or want from your home or another place to make it more useful and/or pleasant (Cambridge and MacMillan dictionaries)

Minimalism – a simple living lifestyle (Wiki)

The definition of minimalism from Wiki is admittedly short and sweet, but it doesn't really encapsulate what minimalism is about. Here are some additional descriptions:

From the book, *Minimalism*: "Minimalism is a tool to eliminate life's excess, focus on the essentials and find happiness, fulfillment and freedom."

From minimalist, Joshua Becker: "The intentional promotion of the things we most value and the removal of anything that distracts us from them," and also, "A lifestyle where people intentionally seek to live with only the things they really need."

From all this we can sum up that minimalism is a focus on the essentials, on what is important to you. It is about culling or curating to the least number of things to create the best effect. Ultimately it is about trying to attain more security, joy, meaning and freedom.

THE MYTHS OF MINIMALISM

I don't know about you, but more happiness, space and control over my life sounds fantastic to me! I love the ideology of minimalism, but I don't like how it is interpreted in practice sometimes. Minimalism can get a bad name because some minimalists take it too far.

Here are some strange, extreme or confusing examples of minimalist behavior and advice I came across when researching this book:

- Put away the all contents of your handbag each night and get them back out each morning.
- Make sure all surfaces are clear including everything on the kitchen and bathroom counter tops.
- Throw it out even if it is the only one you have. (Marie Kondo discarded her only set of stereo speakers, her screwdriver and the last vase in her house!)
- Households only need one towel or two towels per person, depending on what book you read. This was obviously written by someone who hasn't got kids playing muddy sports or had a vomit-bug sweep through the family.
- One book told me to start decluttering in the kitchen,

and another told me to never start off decluttering in the kitchen.

- Don't stock up—one book tried to tell me it was better to buy smaller packets of toilet paper more often than having a few big packs stored away.
- Retain color minimalism—stick to a few bland colors and an almost uniform to what you wear—er, I guess if you want to emulate prison that's a good idea!
- Eat out more—really?
- And the winner is the guy who says he has one single thin towel he uses for drying his body after showering AND wiping the dishes. Join with me here: ewwwww!

The point of decluttering under minimalism is to hold onto your treasured objects and discard the rest, but I think that extreme minimalists compete to trash their most prized, valuable or expensive possessions! Throw away your signed yearbook, your bankbook, a beautiful souvenir from a trip to a beloved country abroad, your last screwdriver / vase / speakers. Bin all your certificates and trophies and while you are at it, get rid of all your photos!

Minimalism is a concept that can be adapted to best suit you and your family. It doesn't mean going without. It doesn't mean not buying anything ever again. It doesn't mean only owning 100 items. It doesn't mean having to give up modern appliances or living in a tiny home.

Please don't let these radical examples put you off starting and sticking to your decluttering project. Really, I had to include them to lighten the mood. All this counsel to decide on your most meaningful and important things and then build a life around them can get fairly heavy. Its good advice, but it's a lot to take on when all you wanted was some guidance about how many handbags you should keep and how to streamline your bookcase!

. . .

Is Minimalism for You?

The concept of minimalism—even if you don't want to label yourself a minimalist—at its core sounds enticing. You can declutter without even thinking about minimalism if you like, but it is helpful to have a background 'Why' to emptying your house rather than doing it for the sake of it. Minimalism provides a purpose behind decluttering.

Utilize the idea of minimalism in a way that is maintainable for you and your family. Minimalism is meant to reduce overwhelm and stress, so if any of the minimalist recommendations cause more pressure, then take them out of the equation. They are not hard and fast rules.

Minimalism may sound vague, but that is awesome as you can adapt it to suit you.

Why I Wrote This Book

I am a fairly organized person and have never thought I was a slob or a hoarder. I am simply a suburban mama who wants a bit more space to breathe. I don't call myself a minimalist, but I do like the concept of minimalism and thought it could help me.

In March 2019 I embarked on a project to declutter my house in one month. I committed to posting something on Facebook every day. It was this accountability that kept me going at times. I wanted the majority of the house that I had control over (i.e.: not my husband's side of the wardrobe or his 'man cave') cleared out. More on how useful accountability and deadlines are in Chapter Five.

Even though I believed I had a handle on my things and that I was generally a tidy person, I had way more stuff than I thought. I uncovered two old video tapes. The last thing recorded on them was from around 2004. For 15 years and at least three house moves, these worthless video tapes had been dutifully carted around.

I read *The Life-Changing Magic of Tidying Up* as I decluttered my home. I liked the simplicity of keeping things that sparked joy, but it left me with more questions than answers:

- What if it is the only one I have of something, but it doesn't spark joy?
- What if something doesn't spark joy but is a family heirloom?
- What if it is something I have to keep like my tax returns?
- What if it's practically useful but doesn't spark joy?
- What if I seriously don't know if it sparks joy?
- Taking everything out and touching it to check if it sparks joy may take a long time, so how do I practically manage this?

This book addresses these burning questions and provides some additional practical advice such as what to do with items you want to discard without sending them to a landfill, how to handle big emotions that may come up and how to continue a minimalist lifestyle in the best way possible.

I wrote this book with the intention that it would be the only book you need to read to declutter once and for all, but if you have read Marie Kondo or any other author in the minimalist space, then it will complement and expand on their advice.

The good news is that I succeeded at decluttering a large portion of my house over that month, but I did it the hard way. This book was written so you don't have to struggle through decluttering like I did.

WE ALL START OUT AS MINIMALISTS

At its worst, attempting simple living can sound like a luxurious first-world problem for people who have realized that owning a lot doesn't lead to any real happiness. After all, it seems crass that we complain about how hard it is to declutter when many people around the world are forced into living with the bare minimum due to poverty and poor socio-economic conditions.

Don't let the fact that minimalism seems elitist or sterile or just plain mad at times stop you from starting. Know that anyone—from the worst hoarder to someone who, like me, identifies with being organized and tidy, can benefit from decluttering. Give it a go—at the very least it will be interesting to see what treasure or trash you discover. And once you declutter you can continue a minimalist lifestyle and not be part of the problem anymore.

After all, as minimalist, Fumio Sasaki, notes, we all come into the world as minimalists. And I would add that we go out of them practically minimalist, too. So why not embrace it through your life as well?

HOW TO READ THIS BOOK

The next two chapters on objections and benefits get your mindset in the right order, then Chapter Five gives you some essential preparation tools before the actual decluttering starts. Chapters Six and Seven answer all your questions about decluttering, provide a game plan and give detailed suggestions to declutter each area of your home. Chapter Eight helps you to tidy and organize the remaining items, and Chapter Nine lists a number of alternatives to discarding your unwanted items in the trash. The final three chapters help those of you who want tips to adopt a minimalist outlook going forward.

It's best to read this book right through before you start decluttering your home and your life. Use it to prepare a plan for decluttering and organizing your home, working out where unwanted items can go and continuing your minimalist journey. Feel free to skim, or even skip altogether, the mega Chapter Seven that goes into detailed suggestions about decluttering each main area of the house until you need it.

As you have now recognized, this decluttering mission is much deeper than just moving stuff out of and around the house. The next two chapters on objections and benefits delve into this mindset piece in greater intensity. Don't skip them—it's important to get your mentality right before launching into the practicalities.

3

NINE OBJECTIONS TO DECLUTTERING

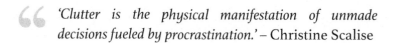

'Clutter is the physical manifestation of unmade decisions fueled by procrastination.' – Christine Scalise

WHY IS DECLUTTERING SO DIFFICULT?

At its core, decluttering is not hard. All you have to do is remove things. The physical act of picking something up and taking it out of a house is something a puppy can do.

What is it about decluttering that makes it so tremendously difficult to actually do?

The need for decluttering is blocked by doubts and concerns. You can rationalize these excuses: "I have no time." You can truly believe them: "I don't know how." And you can defend them even if they don't have much merit: "It cost me a lot of money all those years ago." By looking at your objections you can see they are not brick walls but merely hurdles you need to overcome.

You may be wanting to start decluttering right now, and if so, go for it. However, it is important to get your mindset in the right place so you can declutter only once and in the best way. This chapter on objections and the next one on benefits will help you declutter with a decent mental game in place.

Some of the following objections may ring truer to you than others, so read through them and see what excuses you have voiced most often. It starts with the three universal objections: time, ability and money, and then examines a few more. The chapter concludes with the REAL reason you don't want to declutter.

"I HAVE NO TIME TO DECLUTTER."

Oh boy. The time objection is the most common and, unfortunately, can easily be justified. You are a busy mama. You work, take care of the kids, look after the home. You try to be a good partner, friend, community member, world citizen and even attempt to sleep occasionally. Fitting in a decluttering venture seems like an absurd item to add onto your already overflowing to-do list.

Truth time: yes, you will have to make time to declutter. However, it probably won't take as long as you think, you can fit it into your life in a way that suits you best, and you don't have to do it to perfection. Chapter Six will help you navigate a best approach just for you.

I know the latest binge-watch sensation is more tempting. I know decluttering doesn't sound enjoyable. I know that you are tired. But a one-off decluttering project will take far less time in the long run than constantly rummaging in your handbag, standing in front of your closet not finding a thing to wear and picking up toys from around the house to stuff back into the overfilled toy box.

"I don't know how to declutter."

Remember, the physical act of removing an item from the house is so easy a puppy can do it. What you are really saying is that you are not sure where to start, how to decide on what to keep or remove and what to do with items you decide not to keep.

Truth time: don't worry. This book has you covered. It will give you a clear decluttering strategy including areas to focus on first and questions that prompt quick decisions on what to declutter. It will provide ideas for your personal decluttering goals and how to aim for a finish line. Plus, there is a whole chapter devoted to how to lessen the impact of your decluttering on landfills.

You are in good hands

Look, I don't know your situation, and if you believe you're stuck because of deep emotional attachments or you or someone in your household identifies as a hoarder, then seek out the professional help that is right for you. Why not, though, give it a go and see what you can achieve? Start and you may surprise yourself with where you end up.

"Why throw out something that is valuable?"

You spent money on that treadmill / waffle maker / designer skirt. Keeping items around because you believe they have monetary value seems valid but is actually deceptively flawed thinking.

Truth time: the money you paid for your things is gone. You may have spent a large chunk of your hard-earned money on something expensive. But there is no point thinking of items in terms of their monetary value now. If the only reason you are holding onto something is to prevent negative emotions from not using or wearing it from landing, then let it go and free up your mental space. Feel the feeling of guilt or loss and move on.

If it makes you feel better, arrange to sell it and recoup some of your costs, but don't leave an item hanging around because you have fallen into the sunk cost fallacy—the tendency to continue to invest time, money and energy into a dud.

Chapter Ten will provide some suggestions on how to resist consumer culture so you can be selective with your future purchases to reduce the chance of this happening again.

"I AM KEEPING IT FROM THE LANDFILL."

It seems noble to keep something around to avoid it becoming trash, but it is simply not a good enough reason to hold onto it. There is a myriad of ways that an item can be decluttered and NOT end up in a landfill. Chapter Nine goes into these in depth, but from donating to selling to recycling, freecycling and upcycling (all the 'cyclings'!) there are plenty of opportunities to prevent your unwanted items ending up as garbage.

Truth time: keeping something in your house that you don't want denies others the opportunity to use, wear or enjoy it. Plus, if you keep it too long, it may no longer be desired and then will become landfill fodder when your loved ones have to clear it out after you are gone.

Don't let not knowing the best way to keep something from the landfill stop you from decluttering. Some items will need to be placed in the trash, but what is more wasteful is the unnecessary mental stress of hanging onto things you don't want for far too long.

"MY FAMILY WON'T HELP."

Some people will have partners and kids on board before you can say 'donate'. They will want to be active participants, and your quality family time will involve working side-by-side in a decluttering frenzy. However, for many, YOU may want to declutter, but you get resistance from others in the household.

Truth time: you can't make others declutter their stuff. But you have plenty of scope to do a majority of decluttering on your stuff and in the communal areas of your home even if your family is not on board. You also have the opportunity to show them how great a decluttered space can be. Be the lighthouse and model fun, easy, practical minimalism, and they may change their perspectives. Be patient and let them be empowered to make their own decisions.

If it is your partner that is the trouble area, know that you can't touch their stuff. Explain how important it is for the family. Try to coax your significant other into keeping their things in one or two areas, not all over the place. The 'man cave' was out of bounds during my decluttering rampage, but I made my peace with that knowing I had plenty to sort out with the rest of the house. If you suspect a serious hoarding problem, then gently try and approach the issue without judgment or attack.

With kids, motivate with assurance that nothing they truly love and use will go. Give praise, employ rewards (sticker charts or experiences) and try to make it a bonding time, something fun you do together. Many kids love the idea that the toys they have outgrown will go to a needy child. And everyone likes that it is now easier to find things to play with and tidy up afterwards.

· · ·

"I may use it someday."

Keeping things around because you may need them or use them, or you think you will regret it if you got rid of them is a popular reason to hold onto stuff. It can cover a broad range of items, and because it is so pervasive it seems like a genuine reason. It can apply to duplicates (e.g.: your fifth white t-shirt). It is rolled out when you think you have to hold onto something just in case (e.g.: the washing machine manual). And it is brought up when you think of your 'someday' self when you have the spare time to exercise on that rower / play the guitar / knit.

Truth time: 'It may come in handy' is scarcity mentality wrapped up in procrastination. It is the reason that the storage unit business is thriving. If you add it up, holding onto stuff costs you more in time, energy and money (storing or maintaining) than getting rid of the item and buying another one in the future. I am certainly not advocating you continue throw-away consumer culture ways, but wouldn't you rather buy a new pair of jeans after you lose those last few pounds than hold onto those old jeans you have had for years just in case you fit back into them?

Stores are for stockpiling duplicates of stuff, not your house. The Internet has a wealth of up-to-date and easier to search information, including most appliance manuals.

There is a difference between something being useful and actually using something.

There is a slim chance that you may have regrets if you throw something away. But is this more stressful than keeping something hanging around 'just because'?

This objection is tied up with the money excuse earlier, but it is more than that. When deciding to discard, you are not only saying goodbye to money but to your fantasy self who gets on the rowing machine daily, strums the guitar on quiet Sunday afternoons or finishes knitting that sweater.

If you are not quite ready to give up a particular hobby, then use the item. See if you actually enjoy rowing, playing guitar, or knitting. See if you want to continue trying to improve at it. Close that door if you need to. You have one life, so isn't it better to pursue things that bring you the most fulfillment and that are true to who you really are?

"BUT IT HAS SENTIMENTAL VALUE."

Wanting to keep sentimental items is a good way of telling yourself that decluttering is too hard, as removing them is admittedly very difficult. They have strong emotional attachments that can range from love through to guilt. Sentimental items can come in many forms—that special gift from a loved one, an heirloom from someone dearly departed, kids' artwork, old photos or letters to name a few.

Knowing I was writing a book on decluttering, various friends asked me what to do with their wedding dresses, dried wedding flowers and special wedding gifts from close friends that have never been used. Weddings seem to evoke a lot of tricky emotions!

Truth time: never, ever start decluttering with heirlooms, memorabilia, keepsakes and collections. It is a surefire way to fail. Further—and this may horrify the pure minimalists—don't discard sentimental items at all. At least wait until you have gone through all the everyday items. Sentimental things take up a relatively small proportion of your total household belongings, so just leave them out of your decluttering project, at least initially. Set a date to sort them later if you like.

There are more tips on how best to deal with sentimental items in Chapter Seven, but if you want to start thinking about how to review what to keep, remember this: the item itself is not the holder of the emotion or memory. You can honor the person without the item around. Take a photo of it before you discard it if you want. Plus, don't keep things boxed up just because you feel like you have to keep them. Put photos or kids' artwork in a frame or album, use Grandma's best china or display that collection you have kept stored away all these years.

"I HAVE ALWAYS BEEN DISORGANIZED, UNTIDY, A BIT OF A HOARDER, OR I love to shop."

Your house has a lot of stuff in it and you trip over the clutter now and then. But you think, 'so what?' Alternatively, or in addition to this, you may identify as someone who loves shopping. There are plenty of worse ways to spend your time. What is wrong with 'add to cart' now and then?

Truth time: the more something jeopardizes your identity, the more you will shun it. You won't start or stick to any kind of decluttering regime if your underlying beliefs threaten who you think you are.

What benefit are you generating by holding onto the belief that you are an untidy or disorganized person? Were chores used as a form of punishment when you were young? Can you use the excuse of not being able to locate an item as the reason you don't fix that motorcycle, write that book, or grow that garden? Is it easier to deal with trivial matters concerning your stuff instead of striving for an ambitious goal and possibly failing at it?

Our parents and grandparents often held onto things. A few decades ago, this wasn't a problem as such but a rational response to living through the Depression, rationing and constraints related to poverty and low income. These behaviors have been passed down and you have adopted them. Nowadays, with stores brimming with anything you can buy at any time, you don't need to continue with this default pattern.

As minimalist, Joshua Becker says: "be grateful that we are free to choose to live with less".

Examine your shopping habits. Are you after the next hit, wanting to fill an insatiable hole? Are you worried what others may think if you don't have nice clothes or the latest mobile phone? Are you making up for a childhood in which you had to go without? Is it a reward for all your hard work? Maybe you just like shopping, but why?

There is no judgment here. None. Putting a spotlight onto who you think you are is hard, but living a mediocre life because you think you are destined to as a result of your personality or childhood is far more terrible. You CAN believe different things about yourself to help you transform your home and your life. Anyone can learn to declutter if they want to. And the transformation is usually far greater if you start off believing you can't do this.

The REAL Reason Decluttering is Hard

Having stuff gives us a sense of security, safety and control. Owning things can provide certainty, which is a fundamental human need. My book, *Crappy to Happy*, goes into depth about why this is the case. In brief, we crave certainty due to being hardwired to avoid lack or attack from our caveman days. We also require secure attachment to simply survive as babies. Removing things can bring about uncertainty, which is extremely uncomfortable.

Truth time: everyone has a need for certainty and you can't change that, BUT you can change where your certainty comes from. Instead of certainty from stuff, could it come from putting effort into rich and loving relationships? Instead of craving the security of owning things that prove you 'made it', could you flip it over to garner it from giving things way, from being generous with what you have? Could knowing that you don't have to keep up with the Joneses and instead stay on your own path provide the contentment that possessing things previously gave you?

It is not easy to switch around these ingrained beliefs, especially when what can meet you when you discard things is not any type of certainty but instead a whole barrel load of vulnerability. Holding onto things often means keeping your emotions tied up as your things have meanings attached. Keeping stuff is a way to numb yourself from experiencing negative feelings. Letting go means unleashing emotions of loss, guilt, rejection or fear. It may mean confronting complex feelings related to abandoned love, foolish mistakes or dreams not realized. This is no fun for anyone.

Know that the emotions will pass and on the other side of them are the freedoms that your need for certainty has been seeking all along. The freedom of knowing you don't have to try to control the world. The freedom of understanding that you don't have to hold your emotions at bay, that they will pass and you will feel good again. The freedom of finding out exactly who you are, what matters to you most and then striving for it. But we are getting ahead of ourselves—this will be discussed in the next chapter on the benefits of decluttering.

Phew! You may feel like you have been put through the wringer! You may be thinking that you picked up this book to figure out how many pairs of shoes to keep or what to do with that set of platters that you have never used. How come all of a sudden there is a whole discussion about needs, emotions, vulnerability and fear?

But that's just it, isn't it? You don't need a book to tell you how to declutter. Sure a few tips and strategies come in handy, but you know better than I how best to declutter your own home.

What you need is a mindset shift so when you do declutter, you will KNOW with absolute certainty that your world will not fall apart.

4

NINE BENEFITS OF DECLUTTERING

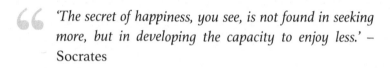

> 'The secret of happiness, you see, is not found in seeking more, but in developing the capacity to enjoy less.' – Socrates

ALL ABOARD

The previous chapter helped you overcome your objections—whether spoken or ingrained—to decluttering. These benefits will not only convince you to start decluttering, but are a handy reference to return to when the going gets tough. They are also useful for convincing reluctant family members to get aboard the minimalism train.

Although there are some material benefits to decluttering, the actual act involves a tangible loss. Your stuff is gone. What it is replaced with is many other advantages, most of which are intangible. You may not be able to see and touch these benefits, but you will soon realize that decluttering is an exchange from which you will gain far more than you will ever lose.

. . .

Less Tidying and Cleaning

Let's start with the easiest benefit—less tidying and cleaning. You won't have to pick up and put away as much clutter. It will now be the rare occasion when you do the most painful thing in the universe—step on a piece of LEGO! You will have the pleasure of walking into a spacious room or opening an orderly cupboard.

Cleaning, although it still needs to be done, won't take as long. I decided to get rid of any of my clothes that needed ironing. Never ironing ever again is something that makes me extremely happy.

Decluttering means less dusting! If that doesn't make you start right away, I don't know what will.

More Time

One of the objections to decluttering is that it takes up too much time. In the short run, it will require a dedicated spell, but in the long run decluttering saves you time. Not only are chores done quicker, but you don't have to search for things, sort through things, maintain things or run as many errands.

As you embrace a minimalist mindset, you will spend less time shopping, make faster decisions at the store and become less distracted by product marketing. What do you do with all this extra time? This will be discussed as further benefits below.

More Money

Minimalism means more money in your back pocket, and this doesn't just mean cash from selling unwanted items, although that is a bonus. People save money by stopping the need to pay rent on offsite storage, by downsizing and paying less home costs and by organizing paperwork to pay bills on time, thereby avoiding late penalties.

Going forward, being happy with what you already have, drastically reducing what you purchase, buying the best quality you can afford and looking after your few precious possessions also helps your budget. As Erica Layne notes in *The Minimalist Way*, an increase in college savings or retirement funds creates "a much more powerful form of stress relief than going to the store ever did."

Enjoy What You Have

One objection not addressed in the previous chapter is the concern that you may get so into decluttering that you throw almost everything away. There are a lot of responses to Marie Kondo's 'spark joy' concept that sum up this worry. For example, "I've now thrown out all the vegetables and the electric bill" or "quits job, deletes landlord's number, burns pants."

Don't worry, you won't trash everything. You are much more likely to keep a whole bunch of stuff that doesn't spark much joy at all. And if you end up with almost nothing, then you can always look to purchase something you will sincerely treasure to fill the space.

The point is, if you declutter well, what will remain are things that you absolutely love and use a lot. There is immense satisfaction in the awareness of knowing and making use of what you have. You will wear clothes that have been lost in the depth of your closet or create a delicious platter on that beautiful serving dish that was hidden in the back corner of the kitchen cabinet. During our decluttering we found an old digital photo frame. I wiped it off, loaded it with our favorite photos and placed it in a prime spot in our lounge. The kids love watching the photos flip by—it is almost better than TV!

BENEFICIAL FOR THE ENVIRONMENT

Living with less means a less heavy environmental impact. Taking up minimalist practices will often mean less food waste as you only buy what you need, less use of electricity or gas as there are fewer appliances and not as much trash in the future as you learn to purchase selectively. Treading a little more lightly on this one planet we call home is the environmental footprint legacy I want to leave to my kids and grandkids.

LESS IS BETTER FOR YOUR KIDS

Talking about children, there is a lot of dubiousness about whether minimalism is the right approach with kids, but there is no need for debate. Decluttering in all its forms is great for our tiny humans. Research shows that extra visual stimuli contributes to sensory overload and is distracting and stressful for kids. Children need the opportunity and space to play freely—as they say, play is a child's work.

Here are a dozen reasons why having fewer toys is better:

- Kids use their imaginations, creativity, ability to dream and resourcefulness more often
- It has been shown that kids will play more with fewer toys as they can easily find what they want
- Perhaps strangely, research confirms that there is often

less arguing and fighting between siblings with fewer toys around

- Children interact more with other kids and adults and learn to be social and pick up on communication cues better
- Deep play with one toy allows better focus, an opportunity to get into flow and develops a longer attention span
- There is more chance kids will go outside in nature and the sunshine, often performing unstructured play, an important part of child development
- As noted above, everyone is happier that there is less to clean, tidy up and that there is a place for everything!
- Children begin to understand that there is a joy to sharing and giving away their things—it invites them to be less selfish
- Fewer toys helps kids to value the toys they have and (hopefully) take responsibility and better care of them
- Not saying 'yes' every time you visit the toy store helps kids understand happiness comes from within, not from the next cool thing
- It gives children a feeling of control as they know what they have and helps them feel secure as you have limits on toy purchasing
- Fewer toys gives kids an opportunity to develop a greater love for reading, writing, scientific or mechanical exploration, or arts and crafts

RELATIONSHIPS IMPROVE

Embracing minimalism as a family is a rebellious act. It means not succumbing to the norm of excess consumption, full schedules and distractions and disputes caused by your stuff. Decluttering can be the start of allowing your family to find out how they connect, rest, work and play best together in their own unique manner.

With less stuff around as a distraction, there is more time to talk. With a reduction in overfilled calendars, there is more time for spontaneous fun. With an emphasis on experiences, not things, relationships feel more connected.

Doesn't that sound wonderful?

You Just Feel Better

Once decluttering is part of your life, you will feel better. You will experience the feelings you were trying to get from buying and owning things on a constant, better quality and more real basis.

As noted in the objections chapter you will feel more in control of your life. With the extra spaciousness, you will feel calmer and more peaceful, like you have room to breathe. With less tension, overwhelm, distraction, decision making and mental stress, you will feel like you have more clarity, focus and energy. With your most treasured possessions remaining, you will feel an increased sense of gratitude and contentment. With your new focus to give away things, you will feel generous. And with not subscribing to the 'buy more and buy now' culture, you will feel good about asserting self-control and your ability to say 'no'.

Allows a Bigger Life

What to do with this extra time, money and energy? It is far easier to get tied up with things and not live a big life. It is easier, but deep down you know it is not what you were put on this planet for.

Don't declutter for the sake of it, but focus on the most important things. It allows you to uncover a better understanding of who you are. It helps you to decide what is of value to you, what you love to do and what inspires you. As Marie Kondo says, "When your room is clean and uncluttered, you have no choice but to examine your inner state."

Here are some suggestions to aid a bigger life. They are all worthy pursuits. Try them out and find what resonates with you:

- Allow yourself to rest, daydream, savor the present, be content with what you have and love simple pleasures once again
- Use improved creativity and ability to get into flow to write that book, finish building the tree house or cook a gourmet meal
- Attempt a long-term goal—try to master something or save for that trip abroad
- Pursue a passion or a dream, something you think will give you immense satisfaction—take a tango class, go on a yoga retreat, try out water skiing
- Volunteer at a charity you believe in—provide your time or money
- Start a side business or participate in a community project
- Spend quality time with your children on fun activities or a challenge together

LIVE YOUR UNLIVED LIFE

Overall, decluttering allows more meaning and happiness into your life, and who doesn't want that? As author, Steven Pressfield says, "live your unlived life."

Don't let your stuff stop you from being engaged with the world around you.

The next chapter introduces you to the five steps in your minimalism journey. It then talks about finding the purpose behind why you are decluttering. It finishes off by providing essential strategies to start decluttering, to keep going and to finish well.

5

WHAT DO YOU REALLY, REALLY WANT?

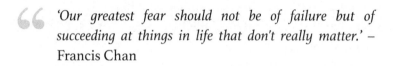 *'Our greatest fear should not be of failure but of succeeding at things in life that don't really matter.'* – Francis Chan

On Your Marks

With objections overcome and benefits highlighted, it feels like the starting gates can be swung open and you can charge ahead with decluttering.

But, whoa, not so fast there, buddy!

This chapter makes sure that you are properly prepared so you can start the race well, continue when the going gets tough and finish it with a smile on your face. Decluttering is not a sprint but a marathon. The intention of this book is to make the long jog as painless as possible.

. . .

Space

Decluttering takes up your precious time and energy, so it has to be worth doing. When I sat down to think about what I really, really wanted for my efforts, I realized that what I craved more than anything else was space.

And, do you know what? The word 'space' makes a mighty good acronym for what you are going to embark upon.

Let's look at the main steps in a minimalist journey. These can happen concurrently, but they are split out here for clarity.

1. Declutter your home – remove or put aside items you no longer want
2. Tidy up and organize your remaining things
3. Decide how to get rid of all the items you don't want (trash, donate, sell)
4. Review and change why, what and how much you buy
5. Embrace minimalist ideas and tools in other parts of your life

Let's abbreviate these five steps using the 'S.P.A.C.E.' acronym:

S - **Simplify** – declutter your home

P - **Place** – organize remaining items, put everything in its place

A - **Act** – take action to remove unwanted and discarded items

C - **Change** – modify your consumer behavior

E - **Embrace** – adopt a minimalist mindset and lifestyle

Know Your Why

As the Spice Girls ask, 'tell me what you want, what you really, really want'. Before you start decluttering and going down the minimalist path, ask yourself WHY are you attempting such a time-consuming, physically tiring and emotionally difficult task.

The trade-off has to be worth it or you will abandon it at the first hurdle.

As I said, I wanted space. Not just to create more spacious areas in my home but space to feel the security, joy, meaning and freedom that comes with embracing minimalism at its core. The definitions of minimalism are quite vague, but its emphasis on paring down my life to the most essential, important and beautiful is very appealing to me.

What would you like less of in your life? Do you want to not feel so hectic, stressed, frustrated, tired on a daily basis? What do you want more of? Do you want to spend more time with the kids, help in the community, have fun, start that side business, nap? What do you value most? Is it freedom or happiness or striving for a more meaningful life?

If you strike on something immediately, then move on to the next part. If you are feeling overwhelmed by the many appealing options, then this quick exercise, adapted from author and wise soul, Martha Beck, may help.

Think of another space, a house, a room or even a spot in nature that is absolutely beautiful. You may have seen it in real life or recall it from a film or a magazine. Create a vivid mental image of the area, or even better, find a picture of it.

Think of three adjectives to describe the place. Choose three words that convey why it appeals to you. Don't ponder this for too long. Is it relaxing, calm, serene? Is it bright, cheery, inviting? Is it sunny, natural, solid?

This living space description exercise not only portrays how you would like your home to be but how you want to feel internally. Use it as a starting point to decide on the purpose behind decluttering. You don't have to write a long-winded purpose statement; three little words will do.

Once you have worked out the reasons behind wanting to declutter, once you have taken a few minutes to get clear on your WHY, take a couple of deep breaths and feel it in your bones.

When you are trying to decide whether to keep that expensive platter you have never used from your dearly departed Aunt Maude, going back to your purpose, your WHY, will help immensely.

GOAL STRATEGIES

This big-picture vision gives you intrinsic motivation, but you need to add in some practical tools. These external tactics assist when internal inspiration isn't quite enough.

Here are the main goal-setting strategies to weave into the decluttering project in order to start well, keep going and finish on time.

START

Here is your permission slip to start. Yes, you haven't read all the instructions yet, but I want you to start anyway. Declutter one space. Choose a small area and put on a timer for, say, five minutes. Declutter your sock drawer, for example. Remove everything from the space. Give it a quick clean, wipe or shake out if you like. Then only place back what belongs there. Put everything else aside for now. We will deal with that later. Walk away from the decluttered area and then reexamine it. How does that feel?

This exercise has demonstrated how much can be done in a small amount of time. It also gave your decision-making muscles a bit of a workout and squashed any remaining limiting beliefs that you can't do this or it will be too hard.

You have done it! You have started.

A small win gives you a feeling of success and is likely to motivate you to continue. It may be hard to believe it now, but the more you declutter, the quicker and more ruthless you will become with your decision making.

Keep it Up

Keeping going is the most important thing. You may need some willpower to start, but you will want strategies in place to keep the momentum going without having to force it. Remember that every little bit helps and if you continue, no matter where you stop, it is not a fail. Use these strategies to make your decluttering efforts, well, as effortless as possible.

Schedule

Dedicate time to your declutter project. Add it into your diary or calendar by assigning or blocking out times or days for it. Even if it doesn't happen as you have diarized, it is much more likely to occur when it is front and center in your calendar. Of course, you may not know how long something will take, but try to do whatever you can in the time you have allocated.

Pro tip: if you can only assign between, say, five and twenty minutes to declutter duty, then put on a timer and stick to the task at hand until it beeps.

ACCOUNTABILITY

When I decided to declutter my home in a month, announcing that I would post something about the challenge every day on Facebook kept me going. Even when I didn't feel like decluttering, I knew I had to do something to keep up the progress.

You may not want to tell a soul what you are doing, but if you think it will help, state it on social media or ask someone to follow up with you. If you are really stuck, ask a close friend to come over to help you declutter. Good friends are not shy to tell you if an item of clothing doesn't suit you, believe me!

My friend and I created a buddy-accountability system whereby we committed to a 10-minute declutter each day for one week to get the momentum going on a tricky area. We texted each other when we started and finished and sent a few virtual high-fives. I concentrated on my filing cabinet, the area that was my nemesis during my one-month declutter. Despite it being a busy time—I had a deadline to finish writing this very book!—it was amazing how much got done in just a handful of 10-minute sessions. I am not quite finished, but I have made significant headway and it wouldn't have happened without accountability.

Pro tip: create a one-week declutter challenge, put it on social media, assign it a unique hashtag and invite your friends to join you.

REWARDS AND INCENTIVES

- Reward – a benefit provided in recognition of achievement and given afterwards
- Incentive – a benefit to motivate an individual to improve his or her behavior, promised beforehand

These are of particular importance on such lengthy projects. Make sure you add in some mini-celebrations as you check off your decluttering in stages. At the very least, mark off your calendar every time you do some decluttering. The streak of Xs is motivating. Use experiences as rewards—watch a film, read a novel, get a haircut or go out for dinner.

Pro tip: Take 'before' photos and then compare them to 'after' photos for a burst of encouragement.

Finish

Even if you have no idea how long decluttering your home could take, put in a deadline. Make it one week or one month or one year from now, but have a set date on the calendar to work towards. I would suggest one to three months tops. Without a deadline, decluttering will drag on until you give up. I didn't finish decluttering everything, but I am elated with how much I got done in just one month.

If it helps, add a bit of accountability into your deadline. Disclose it to people, like I did. Tell your favorite charity you will be dropping off a big box of stuff on a certain date. Or invite friends over for a dinner party, games night, book club or backyard picnic and send out invites for a week after your declutter deadline.

Some decluttering experts suggest that one day you will suddenly come to a point where the amount of stuff remaining is right for you. I really hope that is true, but if not, a foolproof alternative is to have a set finish line in place.

It is about progress, not perfection.

Please don't quit. Do what you can so quitting is not an option. The prize of a life of security, joy, meaning and freedom is too great to not give it the best go possible.

Now that your internal and external motivation is established, we can get down to specifics. The next chapter answers all your burning questions about decluttering and then provides a handy 'Simplify Game Plan' that can be adapted to suit your situation.

ACTION STEP

Decide on your WHY behind decluttering and spend at least five minutes decluttering one small space.

6

SIMPLIFY: Q&A AND GAME PLAN

> *'Have nothing in your houses that you do not know to be useful or believe to be beautiful.'* – William Morris

You Are in Good Hands

There is so much advice as to the 'best' way to declutter that it gets overwhelming and confusing. You must start with the kitchen. Never start with the kitchen. Do it in silence by yourself. Have a decluttering party, invite your friends and play loud music. Do it all in one weekend. Plan to spend the next year decluttering a little at a time. Doesn't it make you want to give up before you even start?

Fear not!

You now know your purpose behind decluttering. You have blocked out time, found some accountability, established how you will reward yourself and put a deadline in place. This chapter will answer your questions so you can quickly choose how to proceed. Plus, it gives a recommended Simplify Game Plan that can be adapted to work for you.

You have everything you need to start decluttering today.

QUESTION: "WHERE DO I START—WHAT IS THE VERY FIRST THING to do?"

Answer: Leave your house. Yes, physically exit your home. Then come back in and walk through every room. Open cupboards and drawers. Peer into nooks and crannies. Look, really look, at your house with fresh eyes. What do you see and feel? What do you want to see? How do you want to feel? This walk-through should take ten minutes, tops, but will help give you an overview of what is required.

QUESTION: "HOW DO I FIT DECLUTTERING INTO MY BUSY schedule?"

Answer: Some fortunate people may have a lengthy period to get stuck into a whole room, e.g.: the kitchen, or a whole category, e.g.: all their clothes. For the rest of us mere mortals, dividing decluttering into chunks of time is the only way to get it done.

Choose a time to declutter that you can stick to. This may involve cobbling together the best way you would prefer to declutter with the reality of your busy life. Even though a whole weekend of uninterrupted decluttering sounds great, it may be more practical to attempt a little each day around your other duties. Marie Kondo suggests early morning is preferable, but for busy mamas it may be late into the evening before a chance to declutter arises.

Most people choose one of or a combination of the following:

- Set aside a focused time, usually anywhere between 5 minutes per day to a couple of hours each week
- Attempt a particular decluttering project (e.g.: the garage) over a day or the weekend
- Take up a challenge, usually to perform a quick declutter of X number of items without thinking too hard, e.g.: take 5 items of clothing out of your wardrobe

QUESTION: "IS IT BETTER TO WORK BY MYSELF OR WITH OTHERS?"

Answer: Again, this is a personal choice and is dependent not only on your preference but on practicalities. The only time you may have to declutter is when the kids are around. You may prefer to declutter by yourself but have agreed to wait until your partner is ready. In practice, some decluttering will happen on your own and some with others.

QUESTION: "WHICH AREA OR CATEGORY DO I START WITH?"

Answer: Even when you schedule in some time, what stops a lot of people is exactly where to start. Do you start small like with one drawer or tackle the most pressing area where the most visible mess resides—often the kitchen table or the entrance way? Do you go room by room—kitchen, bathroom, bedroom, or focus on one category—clothes, books?

Note that you don't have to declutter a whole room at once. In the bedroom, for instance, you can do a few drawers one day, under the bed the next and a shelf in the wardrobe after that. Similarly, you don't have to do a whole category in one go. It's appealing to follow Marie Kondo's categories method, but if you dump all your clothes out, you may never see the light of day again! You could tackle your tops one day then skirts and trousers on another and leave shoes until later.

Start anywhere. Just start!

The only rule is to leave the sentimental items like mementos, keepsakes and heirlooms to last. Begin somewhere else and not with these emotionally-charged items.

QUESTION: "WHAT ARE THE MAIN CLASSIFICATION DECISIONS I WILL have to make?"

Answer: The overall decision for anything you want to declutter is whether to keep it or not keep it. That is all. How we make that decision keeps an entire minimalism industry churning.

No matter what you are decluttering, you need to assign items to one of four classifications. These are keep it, get rid of it, move it to another place in the house and unsure what to do. The items for each of the four can be in contained in separate bags, cardboard boxes or plastic crates, or simply be placed in distinct piles on the floor.

Let's call these four classifications:

- Remain
- Remove
- Relocate
- Really Don't Know

Remain: If you love or use an item, then keep it around. This will be discussed in detail below.

Remove: If something isn't going to be used or you don't love it, consider getting rid of it. The Remove pile will be further sorted into trash, donate, sell, recycle.

Relocate: The Relocate pile is for items you are keeping but that need to go into another part of the home.

Really Don't Know: The whole point of this pile is so you don't break your stride when you are decluttering. Try to allocate into Remain, Remove or Relocate, and if you can't, put the item into this group and move on. Come back later to the (hopefully not too enormous) procrastination pile and keep flexing those decision muscles on the items until they are assigned somewhere. Don't beat yourself up if you are unsure about an item. It is okay to keep it for now. If it helps, jot down any notes, to-dos or follow-ups in a notebook. Or use post-it notes on the items. This is especially handy if, for example, there is a person you have in mind to gift an item to or if something needs repairing.

QUESTION: "WHAT CRITERIA SHOULD BE APPLIED TO KEEP OR TOSS **an item?**"

Answer: The thing to remember during decluttering is you are choosing what stays, not what to discard. It may not seem like there is much of a distinction, but it is about the mindset shift to minimalism and its emphasis on having in your possession only your most treasured items.

Marie Kondo's 'spark joy' method is now very popular. She advises to take each item in your hands, ask if it sparks joy and if it does, keep it. This sounds great in theory but it has its downsides such as what to do with practical items or family heirlooms that don't spark joy. Some people find everything sparks joy, others find nothing sparks joy, and a lot of the time it is hard to even know.

Other decluttering experts provide clear rules. For example, get rid of multiples, get rid of it if it can be easily replaced, rank three similar items and get rid of lowest ranked one or remove it if it has not been used in a year. But where 'spark joy' can be too esoteric, these hard-and-fast directions are too constraining for every situation.

Here is a simple, twofold criteria, summed up well by author and professional organizer, Vicky Silverthorn. She says: "basically it boils down to hanging onto what you need and what you love and ditching the rest."

Take an item and ask:

- **Do you love it?**
- **Do you use it?**

Items that you EITHER love OR use should remain and if they check BOTH criteria, that's even better. All others can be considered for the remove pile. This criteria hits on the emotional part of decision making (love) and the logical part (use).

Love: includes the concept of 'spark joy' but also covers if something is beautiful, if it is well matched to your home, if you have a strong emotional attachment to it or whether it is a cherished part of your history. The question is not 'do you like it?', it is 'do you love it?'—decide accordingly.

Use: is of utmost importance. Note that the question does not ask if you have used it in the past or are planning to use it in the future. It's asking if the item is serving a practical, functional, informational or helpful purpose at the current time. Does it help you save time, make your life easier in some way or perform a number of functions, for example?

QUESTION: "DO I HAVE TO WORK IN SILENCE OR CAN I PLAY music?"

Answer: Again, this is up to you. Do what is more fun or helps keep the momentum up. The only thing I would recommend is no TV, podcasts or audio books as you have to make a lot of decisions and it is too hard to concentrate with these on as well.

QUESTION: "DO I HAVE SAY 'GOODBYE' TO MY OBJECTS?"

Answer: Marie Kondo has added some woo-woo into decluttering by advising us to spend some time saying 'goodbye' to our things. This doesn't have to be out loud. You can acknowledge the item in your head. I actually quite like this as a concept. It provides a brief pause so you can give the item some appreciation for its time with you before you ditch it. If don't like the idea, then don't worry about it. If you think it will take up too much time, then alternatives to individual goodbyes are to write an en masse goodbye letter or just blow them all a kiss as you kick them out the door. If you are just worried about forgetting about it but it has served its time with you, then take a photo of it and place it in the Remove pile.

SIMPLIFY GAME PLAN

Here is the Simplify Game Plan you can adapt to suit you:

- Do a walk-through of your house with fresh eyes

- Schedule a time you can dedicate to decluttering, with others or on your own
- Choose a room or category or part of an area or category to declutter
- Optional: take a 'before' photo of the space as it is
- Pull everything out of the space that you are decluttering
- Optional: give the area a clean when everything is out of it
- Look at or pick up each item and decide between Remain, Remove, Relocate or Really Don't Know and put in assigned piles, bags or boxes
- An item should remain if you love it or use it
- Place all the Remain items back into the space in a tidy way and as they best fit (Chapter Eight provides more tips if required)
- Optional: take an 'after' photo of the space as it is now
- Say thank you or goodbye to the items you put in the Remove pile if that floats your boat
- Give yourself permission to celebrate and include mini-rewards in the process, even if it's just the pleasure of seeing a clean and tidy space
- Rinse and repeat until decluttering is finished

Leave the Remove, Relocate and Really Don't Know piles for now —the best approach for these will be discussed in the following chapters. In brief: take the Relocate items to the where you think they should be in your home and place them there for now. Sort the Remove pile at the end of decluttering into trash, donate, sell, recycle and act accordingly. Address the Really Don't Know pile —either assign it another classification or put it away for a few months and then review it again.

The Simplify Game Plan can be used to declutter any area. If you want guidance on particular rooms and categories, then review the specific section that relates to the area you are decluttering in the next chapter. You don't need to read the next chapter right through. Use it when you need extra help just before you declutter a particular spot.

ACTION STEP

Follow the Simplify Game Plan to declutter your home.

7

SIMPLIFY: ROOMS AND CATEGORIES

> *'If one's life is simple, contentment has to come. Simplicity is extremely important for happiness.'* – Dalai Lama

Big Picture Guidelines

Here are tips and suggestions related to decluttering specific rooms, areas and categories in the home.

It is best to start with your own things first then declutter communal spaces, but note that the areas are not listed in any particular order here. Just because the bedroom is before the kitchen in this chapter doesn't imply you should declutter in that way.

There are assumptions made, such as shoes are in the wardrobe even though in your home, shoes may be in the entrance way. Heck, you may not even have a wardrobe. Utilize suggestions as they best fit.

Always, always, always, look inside every box, drawer and cupboard. Don't assume you know what is in there and that you will want to keep it.

Place all the Remain items back into the space in a tidy way and as they best fit. For extra tips on organizing, read the next chapter.

Regardless of where sentimental items are located, don't make any decisions on them until you have decluttered all the main areas first. Either keep them where they are with a note to sort through later or pull them out and place them into the Really Don't Know grouping.

This is a mega chapter, so it is best to skim through and then when you are decluttering a particular part re-read that section for precise strategies.

BEDROOM

Excluding clothes, shoes and accessories, there shouldn't be a whole lot of things in your bedroom. A bed, some drawers or dressers, perhaps a chair or a TV. In theory, it should be easy to declutter your bedroom. Unfortunately, in reality, bedrooms seem to be magnets for extra stuff. A variety of objects from sports gear to paperwork to holiday decorations can find their way there.

For a bedroom to support rest, it needs to be a serene refuge. Here, whether you love or use an item is important to consider, but overarching those answers is the question of whether the item encourages you to feel relaxed. If the answer is 'no', it should go. It doesn't need to be removed for good but does need to leave the bedroom.

Remember your four classifications—the Relocate pile may grow to be extra-large here. Once the main decluttering in the bedroom is complete, take all items from the Relocate pile and put them where you think they should go. It doesn't matter if that is not their final home. Put them somewhere else and when you start to declutter that area you can sort them properly at that point. Yes, it is double-handling, but when you have a good sleep tonight in your newly decluttered slumber sanctuary, you will be grateful.

Lastly, ask yourself if the TV in your bedroom is in line with your vision of it being a place of rest. Why not remove it—even just for a week—and see if it helps the quantity and quality of your sleep?

CLOTHES

For many of you, your clothes will be what has prompted decluttering to take place. Overflowing drawers, closets stuffed to the brim, clothes piled on chairs, floors and in the laundry hamper... and yet you have nothing to wear!

The Pareto principle stands true with clothes—we wear 20% of our clothes, 80% of the time. I am certainly not telling you to get rid of 80% of your clothes, but the notion is eerily accurate. I have performed two major clothes declutters in the past few years. I took a high percentage of clothes out of my wardrobe then found when I went to declutter a couple of years later, I was STILL only wearing about 20% of the remaining clothes!

There are two ways to simplify your clothes: all at once or section by section. You can dump all your clothes out on your bed and go through them one by one until you are done. The subsequent mountain of clothes could horrify you into making some quick declutter decisions or may overwhelm you into complete inaction. Alternatively, look at one drawer or one type of clothing —underwear then tops then trousers, at a time. This can be less stressful but will not give you an understanding of what you have, plus it can take longer.

Either way, take all the clothes out of the area you want to declutter and decide between Remain, Remove, Relocate and Really Don't Know. Then put the Remain pile back. Don't worry about best hanging or folding methods for now—this will be discussed in the next chapter.

Some experts advise to only have this or that remaining. One book said I should have a cashmere blazer and a pencil skirt in my wardrobe, items of clothing I have never owned in my life! Others tell you to cut back on multiples, remove anything not worn in a year, discard items not part of key outfits or those that are out of style.

Don't worry about those rules. Instead ask, as always, if you love it or use it. If you are not sure if you love or use an item of clothing, then ask these questions:

- **Love** – Do I look great in it, is it flattering, in my colors, does it fit well?
- **Use** – Do I wear it often, is it comfortable, does the fabric feel nice, do I miss it if it's in the wash?

Still not sure? Try it on! At least pick it up and feel it. If it feels uncomfortable, scratchy, sits funny or has a rip or stain you don't want to deal with, then toss it.

The only rule is that all your remaining clothes must fit back into your drawers and closet properly, not stuffed to the brim. You are allowed to keep all five white t-shirts or any number of little black dresses. You don't have to get rid of things that are worn, stained or have holes if you love wearing them.

You are allowed to keep things that don't fit but you still love. If you have a goal to fit into something and your clothes help you striving toward that goal, then keep them. If you have a couple of dusty old pairs of jeans from your teenage years that are staying around in the hope you could squeeze back into them one day, it may be time to ditch them.

It is also acceptable to keep things that don't suit your lifestyle now but may do in the future. If you wear more casual clothes now you are home with the kids, you don't have to get rid of your all your tailored work suits. But if you can't see yourself wearing that expensive pin-striped outfit even if you return to full-time employment, give it away now and let others get some wear out of it.

Be honest about the clothes that need mending or repairing. Will you sew that button on or fix that hem? If so, keep it around— leave it in the relocate box for now to remind you to take action on it. If not, remove it without a second thought. If you have one of a pair of socks, either embrace wearing odd socks or throw it away. Don't keep an odd sock around in the hope the other one will miraculously return one day. It won't.

Apply the same criteria to shoes, handbags, purses, accessories and jewelry (unless it is sentimental—leave that until later). Be radically honest with shoes especially. If they pinch your feet, make you feel unstable or the soles are worn through, consider putting them in the Remove pile.

Lastly, have fun. Put on your old prom dress even if the zip doesn't go all the way up. Walk around and try not to topple over in those killer heels. Model every silk scarf or purse you have in front of the mirror.

Note: For the kids' bedrooms and their clothes, repeat the steps above. All that advice applies, plus you can keep a box or two of hand-me-down clothing stored away if you will have use for them in the next few years. The main difference is instead of decluttering on your own, you may want to involve the kids. This is dependent on how old they are, whether they care about their clothes and how likely it is they will stay on task.

LIVING AREAS

This communal space may be more than one room and have different names: living room, family room, sitting room or lounge. Regardless, the game plan stays the same. Use the four classifications to sort through items and the 'love it or use it' criteria to make decisions.

The difference here is that some of the items you make decisions on may be large, a lounge suite, coffee table, bookshelf or entertainment system for example. Of course, these won't fit into a Remove box, but you can still physically remove the item, even if you need some help to lift it.

Look at the biggest items, like the furniture, in the room first. Then review the other items such as ornaments, CDs, DVDs, books and toys. Books and toys will be discussed below. With ornaments consider taking them away for a week and seeing whether you like the space and ease of dusting more than the decorative item. For CDs and DVDs, is there a way to store them in a hidden cabinet such as a drawer beneath the coffee table or the bottom of the bookcase or take them out of the lounge altogether? Put them in a box or container. Perhaps even give them away. Most films and music can be played via digital download these days.

Lastly, do you need a TV cabinet at all? Consider wall mounting the TV and removing another bulky piece of furniture altogether.

. . .

BOOKS

For some of us, our books represent fond memories of long afternoons reading silently and wonderful recollections of losing ourselves in a favorite story. Books are sturdy and trustworthy, like true friends, and you don't want to kick your besties out of your life, do you?

If you are a real bookworm with a deep attachment to your bookcase, then you may want to leave simplifying your books. But I bet even the most dedicated book lover could go to their bookcase and pull out 20 books to give away without too much effort.

When I decluttered my books, I was surprised to find that my bookcase didn't actually look that different once I put back all the books I decided to keep, despite a huge Remove pile. That was because I had been stuffing books behind other books for years! I basically started with double the number of books that my bookcase should be holding! Be honest with yourself about how many books you actually have.

Gather together all your books—the ones on your bookcase as well as those stacked on your bedside table and those stored elsewhere. Take them off the bookcase and place them all on the floor. Go through them one by one and decide if you love it or use it. If the answer is 'no' place in the Remove pile.

It is a good idea to shift your mindset about giving away books. Effectively, you get to share the joy of the book if you sell, donate or give it away. A book doesn't need to be kept to retain the memory of how it made you feel good. Most books are easily replaced these days and you can always buy the eBook version to reduce physical space required to store it.

Books are fun things to remove from your house. Know that barely any will end up as trash. You can give them to your friends or family, donate them to a second-hand book shop or charity store, or offer them to libraries, hospitals, prisons or schools. There are so many ways books can be given away and then picked up and loved by someone else. More on this in Chapter Nine.

If you are not sure if you love or use a book, these sub-criteria will help you decide:

- Keep a book IF, even if you won't read it again, is it a favorite and you adore having it on your shelf
- Keep a book IF it has a special significance for you, e.g.: it is rare, out of print, a classic or signed by the author
- Remove a book IF you will never start reading it, finish reading it or read it again
- Remove a book IF you wouldn't happily recommend or lend it to someone
- Remove a book IF it is an out of date reference or travel book or a book you won't use such as a cookbook with recipes that don't fit your culinary tastes

How many books should you end up with? As many as you have shelf space for and no more. Like your wardrobe, keep enough books so they fit nicely on your bookcase. You can have empty space on a shelf too—your books don't have to be squeezed in. Marie Kondo infamously spoke about the fact that she only owns about 30 books at a time, but there is no set number to aspire to.

Lastly, try not to read books during your allocated declutter time to decide whether to keep them or not. You will fall into a story blackhole and never finish decluttering! Leave reading as a nice reward at the end of today's decluttering efforts.

KITCHEN AND DINING

A kitchen should be a joy to cook in and the kitchenware contained there should be easy to clean and put away. Wouldn't you love to waltz into your kitchen and easily prepare dinner without moving stuff to the side or trying to locate the ingredient or pot you most need?

The problem with the kitchen is where to start. It all seems so overwhelming. All that food. The cabinet full of glasses and cups. Those platters languishing in the back corner of a cupboard. Rarely used kitchen appliances stacked wherever there is room.

To start, get rid of the visible mess, like the clutter on top of the kitchen table and counter top. I am not talking about the toaster, leave that for now. I am zeroing in on the school work, junk mail, keys, bags, toys and other things that find their way to the counters in your kitchen and dining area and then tend to stay there. Most of this can be tipped into the Relocate crate and dealt with later.

What should be left on a kitchen counter top? I can't tell you how many books I read that said they should be completely clear. Personally, I think that is a ridiculous level of perfection that can be left for open homes and design magazines. On our good days, our counter has a jug, toaster, fruit bowl, knife block, cutting boards, food scrap bin for compost and cooking oils. I have even managed to sometimes put away the dish rack, which makes me feel like a minimalist rock star! I guess I could try a bit harder—oils could go in a cupboard and Marie Kondo suggests food scraps for compost could be stored in the freezer. However, I have the balance right for me. Choose whether it is more stressful for you to see something on the counter or to heave it out of a drawer or cupboard each time you need to use it.

It is unlikely you can get the kitchen decluttered in one go, so take it in sections. Below are tips for the main areas—apply them in the order that makes sense to you. Have your four boxes at the ready and your decision-making muscles flexed.

Pull out everything from an area, give the empty space a wipe down and start simplifying. In the kitchen, it is not really about the 'love it' criteria but a ruthless review of whether or not you use it. Overall, if you will use it AND you can find a place for it inside a cupboard, cabinet or drawer without cramming it in, then it is perfectly acceptable to keep it. There is no expectation to have to eat out as a result of bare cupboards!

FRIDGE

First clear the outside of the fridge. Take off the magnets, kids' artwork, reminders, calendars, photos and school certificates stuck to the doors. Be very selective about what goes back on again—maybe just one new favorite drawing or a special award. Perhaps keep the door free of stuff for a week and see if you like the new look.

Next, check the top of the fridge. This seems to be a place that is missed but holds all kinds of clutter. Remove it all. There has to be a better place for whatever is up there.

Now, finally, you can open the fridge. Pull out everything including food on the door shelves and in the produce bins. Are you planning to eat it soon? No? Remove it. It is optional to clean when decluttering, but I find a good scrub of the inside of the fridge is long overdue, at least in my home. Repeat this process for the freezer.

PANTRY

Take all the food out and put back only what you truly will eat in the next month or two. Will you ever use that five-spice mix, that can of peas or that packet of buckwheat you bought on a whim when you went through a healthy phase? Use up food in some inventive ways if you like and then endeavor not to buy those things again. You can have a lot of cans, jars and packets, but you unless you are prepping for the zombie apocalypse, try to pare down to a reasonable level. Many homeless shelters and churches gratefully accept non-expired food. It doesn't have to go in the trash unless it is past expiration date, and even then, it is worth checking.

EATING AND DRINKING EQUIPMENT

The main rule here is, will all the glasses, cups, plates, bowls and cutlery fit in their designated areas? If you have too much of one thing, consider donating it. Will you ever use six sets of mugs or 20 champagne flutes? If you have a party you can hire or borrow as needed. And don't 'save' the best china or dish set for that one annual dinner party, start using it today.

KITCHEN APPLIANCES, GADGETS AND COOKING EQUIPMENT

Will you ever use the food processor, pestle and mortar, waffle maker, juicer, ice-cream maker, steamer, bread maker, electric wok, yogurt maker? If you don't know, then pull it out, find a couple of things you can make with it and attempt them in the next week. If it is easy to use and clean, makes yummy food, or makes your life easier, then keep it. If not, it has to go.

For pots, pans, large dishes, platters, baking equipment or silverware the question is not only will you use it, but how many do you really need? For most things, one for cooking with, one in the wash and one spare is more than enough.

OTHER

For most other things in the kitchen, keep them around if they are being used and fit in their space. Toss very worn tea towels and recycle plastic containers without lids.

Lastly, sort out that junk drawer—you know that one drawer in the kitchen where all sorts of stuff ends up—batteries, old keys, rubber bands, rolls of baking paper, coasters. Use the stuff or toss it. Enjoy the pride and ease of opening a near-empty drawer.

BATHROOM

Take out everything from the drawers, cupboards, vanity or cabinet in your bathroom. Give the empty spaces a clean. Only put something back if you will actually use it. Like the kitchen, if you are not sure if you will use that half-finished green eye shadow, body bronzer, dry conditioner, keep it close at hand and attempt to use it in the next week or two.

Most wet makeup such as foundations, mascaras and lip glosses have a shelf life of 12 months or less. Dry makeup such as eye shadows should be kept no longer than two years. Perfumes may last three years, but their fragrance deteriorates after that. Medicines need to be reviewed and disposed of properly if they are past expiration or no longer needed. Check local guidelines whether it is okay to place prescription medicines in the trash or whether it is better to return them to a pharmacy or police station.

If there are hair, teeth, shaving or body cleaning products that are unopened and won't be used, consider donating them to charity. Places like domestic violence shelters usually have great need for bathroom and grooming supplies. Unused makeup would be welcomed by charities that support women recovering from cancer or trying to enter the workforce. More on this in Chapter Nine.

Lastly, it is okay to have multiples. I like a bulk supply of toilet paper at the ready. But ask yourself how many hair brushes, bottles of moisturizer and fancy soaps do you really need?

Toys

Now that you know fewer toys are better for your kids (re-read that section in Chapter Four if you need to), the main issue with decluttering toys is whether to involve your children. For young children you can probably declutter without their input. Older kids may want a say on what to keep.

If you do involve your little ones in the toy declutter, make it fun. It is a good opportunity to spend some quality time together, show them the benefits of giving something away and reassure them that their most treasured toys will remain.

Remove toys no longer loved or used, especially those that are missing pieces, broken or outgrown. If you are unsure whether the toys you want to remove will be missed, then pack them away for a while and see if anyone in the household notices their absence or requests them. Some families put containers of toys on permanent rotation. Each week or month a box gets put away and another replaces it. This keeps toys fun and exciting but takes extra work.

If you are not sure what toys to keep, then usually the classic ones are the best. In our house, picture books, LEGO, train sets, toy cars, board games and art supplies are favorites.

Lastly, be aware of the difficulty of getting rid of soft toys. They are cute and cuddly and can invoke a lot of emotion. Don't look them in the eye or you will never part ways!

Home Office and Paperwork

Paper, paper everywhere! For a modern society that is supposed to be in the digital age, we are swamped with paper! You may not have a home office, but these tips apply even if you currently use the kitchen table.

Desk

Clean everything off your desk, give it a quick wipe and only put back what you actually need. A desktop with just your computer, laptop or tablet sitting on it plus perhaps a notebook or diary and a pen is the goal here.

Stationery and Supplies

Sort out all the stationery and office supplies in your drawers and cupboards. Is your stockpile of rubber bands, paperclips and envelopes too large for one family to get through this century? Charities and schools would welcome your functioning multiples. Review your electronics. Do you still have a fax machine, a broken shredder or a printer that has been out of ink for three months? Remove or repair it.

. . .

PAPERWORK

Address all the visible clutter—all the paperwork that is just out. The junk mail, bills to pay, documents to file and school notices. Place those in one of three piles: action, file, recycle. Put all those papers that need actioning in an in-tray of some kind, file those that have been sorted and place the remainder in the paper recycling.

At some point, and this doesn't have to be part of your initial decluttering efforts, tackle your filing container, box or cabinet. I spent a few hours inside my filing cabinet during my declutter month and it nearly broke me. I am attempting to finish off the declutter in there with a 10-minute per day strategy (see Chapter Five). When you find printed-off forwarded email jokes from 2002, you know you have a filing clutter problem!

Ask yourself if you really need to file something. If you have paid the bill, does it need to be filed? Do bulky appliance manuals need to remain when you can usually find them on the Internet? How long do you need to keep receipts for? If you are not sure if you should still be holding onto tax returns or other important documents, check with your local authority.

DIGITAL

Don't forget a digital declutter. Back up your computer before you start. Tidy up your electronic folders and move stuff off your computer desktop into the appropriate folder or trash it. Empty the trash, too! There are more digital decluttering tips in Chapter Eleven.

Lastly, junk mail is junk. The clue is in the name. Remove it from your life forever.

. . .

STORAGE

There are so many storage areas and so many types of items that can be stored that it is impossible to include everything in this section. Here are the main things to consider when decluttering cupboards, attics, cellars/basements, garages and sheds.

First, put aside any sentimental items such as kids' artwork, collections or old photo albums and review those last. There are so many other items to focus on, you don't need to be bogged down by any emotionally-charged decisions.

Second, look at the space you have and decide how much of it you want to be taken up by stuff, especially items in boxes and containers you barely look in or use. You may have an enormous basement, but does it have to be filled with dusty boxes? Wouldn't you rather redesign the space into a craft / music / fitness / games room? Or you may have no space but lots of stuff—garages are meant to be for parking cars in, people!

For the linen cupboard, I don't subscribe to the notion of a certain number of towels per person. Keep the towels that you use and that also fit nicely on the shelf space you have. Same goes for sheets, pillow cases, blankets and bed covers. It is okay to have extras, just don't cram them all in.

Use the 'love it or use it' criteria and apply it mercilessly on tools, sports and recreational equipment, hobby gear, garden furniture, yard equipment, craft supplies, sewing kits (including buttons), decorations, rain and snow gear, electrical cables and vases. Same goes for your car—give that a good going over. It can be a second home to store receipts, change, toys and clothes.

Lastly, decluttering an area like the garage, basement or attic could be made into a party. Invite some loved ones, entice them with promises of snacks, crank up the music and devote an afternoon to a Simplify Soiree.

. . .

SENTIMENTAL ITEMS

We have finally reached the top of the declutter mountain. We have trekked uphill, panting and sweating and now we are at the simplify peak. All that hard work strengthening your decision-making muscles will enable you tackle the most difficult of categories—all your sentimental items. You must be amped!

Er, this advice goes against conventional minimalism, but you don't need to declutter your sentimental items at all. You really don't! You have performed a major feat decluttering the rest of your home so you can give yourself a break.

Especially if they take up a negligible physical space and not much mental bandwidth, don't worry about getting rid of mementos, keepsakes, memorabilia, collections, heirlooms, special gifts or kids art and awards for now. If you like, put a date in the calendar to sort in one, three or six months time.

If and when you do want to get stuck in, here are some top tips for decluttering sentimental items without being emotionally scarred. First, take your time. This is not an area where a 'jettison five items in five minutes' challenge is a great idea. Give yourself time to decide whether you really love an item or if you are only keeping it out of guilt, politeness or some historic sense of duty.

Ask yourself if you could use the item. Have the collection out on display, eat with that fancy silverware or wear that pearl necklace handed down from your great-grandmother.

Remember that your memories are not stored in an object but in your heart, and sometimes letting go of the past helps create an optimal future.

Here are some suggestions that may assist your decision-making:

- Determine in advance how much space or how many boxes you are going to allow yourself to store and stick to that
- Maintain a special memory box for yourself and each of your kids and be vigilant about what is placed in there
- Before you remove an item, take a photo or write a little note about it to help you remember it
- For things like kids' artwork or collections, keep a representative handful rather than all of them
- Digitalize personal videos, boxes of photos, kids' artwork or school and sports certificates if you want
- Ask family members to help you, especially for heirlooms and old photographs, this is especially important if you don't want to continue to burden another generation with memorabilia
- Give yourself time to enjoy or use something for a while and then allow yourself a guilt-free permit to remove it if you decide it is not right for your home

KID STUFF

Kids are clutter makers! And they are your kids—how can you get rid of their artwork, craft creations, school work, certificates and awards? Well, you can if you want to. Kids are usually not as attached their stuff as you might think, so get them involved if you like. Remember keeping everything is like keeping nothing as it doesn't show what is most valuable to you.

It helps to have a system. This is the 'Display – Box – Discard' method:

- Display – Exhibit the art piece or award for a while. Put

art or certificates on the fridge, stick them on a special
wall or hang them on a wire line.

- Box – Put away school work, art and certificates, and at
  the end of each year or when the box is full, review and
  pare down to the best.
- Discard – Remove the least favorite items once they have
  been boxed for a while—take a photo of them before
  you discard if you want.

If you have a prolific artwork creator, gift some of your child's
best paintings to a grandparent or family member. If there are
volumes of artwork coming home, instead of boxing it up, think
of other ways you could enjoy it, even for a brief period. A friend
uses the copious amounts of large kindergarten drawings that
arrive each day as wrapping paper!

For special pieces of art, frame them. A mosaic of a lot of colorful
pieces together looks great. These days you can digitize the best
art. You can take a photo of it to remember it. You could set up
email accounts for your kids and post images of their creations in
there to look at when they are older. Or you can create a photo
book or other memorable souvenir from their pictures.

MEMENTOS, KEEPSAKES, MEMORABILIA AND COLLECTIONS

I loved looking through old letters, postcards, ticket stubs and
greeting cards when I decluttered and I was glad I had kept them.
They only take up a couple of shoe boxes and sit nicely on top
shelf in my wardrobe so I don't mind them hanging around.

It is a very personal decision whether to keep things like your
school awards, sports trophies, yearbooks, items from past
relationships, special memorabilia from childhood, letters, cards,

postcards, wedding things, special baby items, collections and treasured souvenirs.

You can take photos before removal, keep a few of the best, display them or use them. How you go about that depends on the item. Some of you will be happy to digitalize and then ditch your school certificates. Others will choose a handful of the most unique items to remember your wedding day and remove the rest. A review of baby things is often good to pare down to the most special items and gift out the rest so other parents can benefit from them.

If you are unsure, it is okay to take some time to decide. I have a stamp collection that is not only stamps I collected but ones that got handed down to me. I am not sure what to do with it, but I am fairly sure my kids won't want it—I doubt they know what stamps are!

HEIRLOOMS, INHERITED ITEMS AND SPECIAL GIFTS

You really don't have to keep an item just because it is an heirloom or a special gift. The person will not be searching for it when they are around at your house, especially if they are now dearly departed! They would want you to love and use it, not keep it out of some misplaced sense of guilt.

Heirlooms may be valuable, so you could contact a museum or historical society to see if they would like it. Or you could sell them and buy something that reminds you of the person or donate the money to their favorite charity.

PHOTOS

There are two types of photos: physical and digital. For digital photos, have a system to upload, sort and back up regularly. Delete blurry photos or excessive multiples before uploading to keep the numbers down. They should be automatically sorted into date order at the very least. If your online photo system allows, indicate your favorites. Print and display the very best. I create a calendar with some of the best photos from the year, which makes a great Christmas gift for family members.

You will also have physical photos. These can be yours or ones handed down from other family members. They can be in boxes or albums or a combination of them. What do you do with all your old photos? Some suggestions seem quite harsh: ditch any photo you don't know the person in. Some seem quite cumbersome: review and scan to digital every single photo. Only you will know what you really want to do and how much time you want to dedicate to sorting through photos.

Here is one suggestion you can do with your family—have an afternoon or a few evenings of looking and sorting. If photos are placed neatly in albums, leave them. Sort through loose photos and remove ones of dubious quality that are blurry, badly lit, or skewed. Discard or give away photos that have many duplicates. Write on the back any names or dates if you know them. Sort them into some semblance of chronological order if that is possible. Consider putting them into physical albums, scanning them or containing them in a box.

While you are at it, review the photos in frames and on your walls. Can you swap out some photos? Give them an update or a refresh? Or will taking them away altogether improve the space?

Lastly, no matter what rules, advice or strategies are detailed here, if your heart breaks at the thought of tossing the sentimental item, keep it no matter what.

The next chapter will provide suggestions to tidy and organize so that everything that remains has a place in your now decluttered home.

Action Step

Declutter each area using the Simplify Game Plan and the specific tips in this chapter.

8

PLACE

> 'A place for everything, everything in its place.' – Benjamin Franklin

PAT ON THE BACK

Put one hand straight up in the air, bend it at the elbow and give yourself a pat on the back. Nice work! You have decluttered your home, or at least started. If you followed the Simplify Game Plan, then you will have returned the Remain items tidily to their spaces and also put the Relocate items where you believed was the best place for them.

You may not even need this chapter!

But what if after you decluttered you still don't think there is enough space to store all your items? Perhaps you are not sure if you folded your clothes the right way. Do you need labels? Have you attempted to relocate something and it doesn't fit in its new home? Are you allowed to buy extra storage containers? And what do you do with the Remove and Really Don't Know piles?

It is time for another question and answer session.

"How should I organize all my items?"

Follow Marie Kondo's advice here and place all related items in the same area. Try to contain toys into one or two parts of the house, each person's clothes should be in their own drawers or wardrobe, and miscellaneous items such as stationery, electric cables and crafts should be grouped with other stuff that is similar. Shoe boxes or plastic crates are great for this and some people swear by drawer dividers. And yes, everything needs a designated space of some sort, not the kitchen counter or the middle of the hallway.

If it doesn't have a proper home in your home, what is it doing in your home?

During my declutter month, I discovered that board games were stored in three different areas. After decluttering, I located an almost empty cupboard and placed all the board games in one place. The kids love the fact that they can go there and easily find a game to play. Streamlining our board games seems like an insignificant thing, but it has made our lives better.

Don't worry if you are not sure if it's the 'right' way. Do it YOUR way.

"Should I use labels?"

That is up to you. If maintaining a labeling system is easier than searching for the thing you want because you don't know what drawer, cupboard or box it is in, then label away. It is prudent to label long-term storage boxes, but for day-to-day items, that can be at your discretion.

"What is recommended if what remains still doesn't fit?"

There are a number of different options here. First, have you thoroughly removed everything? Double check if anything more can go. When you have practiced this over a period of time, you tend to get more ruthless.

Next, try not to purchase any more storage solutions, especially expensive or large ones. Work with what you have. Sometimes, to fit things in, all it takes is a few hooks on the wall, an extra basket, carton or box or better use of drawer, hanging or shelf space.

That said, going forward, purchasing furniture pieces that have storage built in is wise. Don't run out and rejig all your storage now! But if furnishings need replacing, then beds with drawers underneath, ottomans and footstools with hollow space and coffee tables with discrete shelves are all great options.

If you put everything in a space but it doesn't look tidy, then consider the best type of organization system for the item. We have a few small, cube-like shelves for the shoes that are in the garage as we found we were tripping on a pile every time we tried to leave the house. Yes, it is another thing we bought, but it keeps the shoes contained and out of the way.

"My clothes still don't look right – any tips?"

In your drawers and shelves, you certainly do not have to learn the Japanese art of folding, but please go ahead if that will help.

Look for videos on YouTube and fold away to your heart's content. It is not covered here.

Choose to hang clothes in a way that makes sense in your closet. Either put outfits together, have similar colors grouped or go from shortest to longest length or lightest to heaviest fabric. Hooks for handbags, scarfs and belts are often helpful in here.

"The toys seem scattered all over the house—what do I do?"

Have a dedicated area or two for toys. Encourage the kids to place toys back in those places. If you have a playroom, great, but don't fill it up—leave some space for playing. Alternatively, have a section of the living room or the kids' bedrooms that toys are stored in. Low level cubes, bookcases and trunks are good options to contain toys—easy for little ones to see what they like, grab things and put away without too much of a fuss. It helps to have different types of toys in separate spaces—books on one shelf, puzzles on another, cars in one container, and Barbies in a separate box.

"Is there a best way to organize my kitchen?"

For non-food, the best way to sort out kitchen items is to place well-used and day-to-day items at the front and rarely-used or special occasion items at the back. Your favorite mug should be front and center. That gravy boat or crystal bowl you use during the festive season can be stored in the back corner of the highest cupboard. Group similar items in one place—large cutlery all in one drawer and pots stacked together.

In the pantry, food crammed in or languishing at the back will not be seen or eaten. Stock up if you like, but make opening the pantry an inviting, not overwhelming, experience. Food items can be grouped with others like them with seasonings and spices in one place, canned food together and baking items placed with each other.

"My paperwork still looks like a mess—any suggestions?"

Create three distinct areas for your papers: action, file, recycle. For incoming papers that you need to action, an in-tray, shallow container, plastic folder or a designated surface to pile these on is sufficient. Allocate a time each week to sort through your paperwork.

Once actioned, decide to file or recycle. Have a box for paper recycling and empty it on a regular basis. For filing, create a system that works for you. If you have to have an 'out tray' as you have no time for filing at the time, so be it, but attempt to keep that as low as possible. Place all documents you want to keep in a filing cabinet, file drawer, binder or box to keep documents secure. Review these long-term files once per year and remove anything no longer required. As for what categories to file in and what exactly to keep, I leave that up to you.

Going forward, go paperless as much as possible to reduce the influx. Ask for bills, statements and invoices to be sent via email. Cancel subscriptions to newspapers and magazines and read them online. Unsubscribe or ask to be taken off junk mail lists. Use a scanner or take digital photos to save items rather than printing or clipping. Think carefully before printing out anything.

"What do I do with all these electrical cables, chargers and plugs?"

If you don't want to throw them out, place all the mysterious cables, attachments and devices in one box and put them up high in a cupboard somewhere. You will never use them, but you may feel better knowing that they are all stored together in a safe spot. Same goes for miscellaneous small items that you might need such as keys and batteries.

"Do I have to fill up each cupboard or drawer?"

Absolutely not. Author, Gretchen Rubin, has one empty shelf as it makes her feel good. The conventional wisdom is loading an area to between 70% and 90% full—enough so the space is used well but not so much that it is all stuffed in.

"Am I allowed multiples and extras?"

Absolutely. As long as there is enough room for them.

"What do I do if I really don't know whether to keep some things?"

First, pick up the item again and ask yourself if you will use it or if you love it, and make a decision. If you are still not sure, then place it in a procrastination container and set a date in your calendar when you will review the items, no later than six months from now. Allow yourself this indulgence to finish your declutter project for the time being.

The only rule here is to try and keep this down to a couple of boxes maximum. If you have a whole room of Really Don't Knows, you have not embraced decluttering the right way. It is practically guaranteed that in six months you will open your procrastination boxes and think, 'Why on Earth was I keeping all of this junk?'

"IT ALL KIND OF LOOKS A BIT BARE NOW—WHAT DO I DO?"

Enjoy the space! You may not be used to it, so give it a bit of time. If it helps, add a pocket of color here and there to brighten it up. Hang up a picture. Frame some of the kids' artwork. Or buy a fresh bunch of flowers and place them in that vase that usually gathers dust under the kitchen sink.

ESTABLISH ROUTINES

'Fantastic!' you say. The house has been decluttered and organized. How do I keep it that way? The kids come home and suddenly it looks like a tornado hit. Does that mean I have failed? No. What it means is that you are normal.

There is absolutely no way you can maintain a perfectly pristine home, so don't worry about trying.

The good news is, now that there is less stuff, tidying up is much easier. If you establish a few easily maintainable routines, your house will look spotless in no time. The aim is to keep surfaces and floor areas as clear as humanly possible. Good habits and routines sound boring, but they make your life better.

Here are some recommendations:

Entrance way – Have shelves or cube spaces for bags, backpacks, equipment and daily footwear plus hooks for jackets and umbrellas. Use a container or hook for keys. Have an in-tray for mail and papers at the entrance way or train family members to deposit them into the in-tray in the office or wherever it sits.

Daily pick up habit – Spend a few minutes (by yourself or as a family) at the end of each day retrieving things from where they lie and placing them back to their designated spot. Or have a box where all stray items end up, which encourages everyone to find and relocate their own things.

Shopping – Take purchases out of bags and packaging, take off any price tags and put them away when you get home from the store. Have a place to put away the bags (a hook or a drawer) to use again.

Handbag – On a regular basis, at least once per month, clean out your handbag. It is amazing the amount of receipts, cards, toys, small clothing items and makeup end up in there. Keep the amount in your handbag to a minimum—your shoulder will thank you for it.

Newspapers and magazines – Once you're finished reading, put them in the recycling box straight away. Scan or take a photo of an article if you want to keep it.

Lastly, spare change should end up in a wallet not in pockets or down the back of couches! Decluttering saves you money in a variety of ways, including this one!

KEEP THE CLUTTER OUT

Be vigilant with what is already in your home. Review regularly if things are being used or if you still love them. Many families have a 'donation spot', a clearly identified bin, box or corner in the house somewhere. If things are no longer wanted, they can be placed there. Check the items to make sure no one's favorite toy was put in there by a disgruntled sibling, and then drop them off at your favorite charity organization next time you are nearby.

Now that the house is tidier, you will be more inclined to keep it that way. Chapter Ten delves into changing your consumer behavior so you buy less. The next chapter provides all the ways clutter can be removed without it ending up in the trash. Here is the help you need to finally sort your Remove pile.

ACTION STEP

Make sure the Remain, Relocate and Really Don't Know piles have been put away.

9

ACT

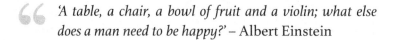 *'A table, a chair, a bowl of fruit and a violin; what else does a man need to be happy?'* – Albert Einstein

HAPPY ANNIVERSARY

There is an Internet meme that states, "Happy two-year anniversary to the bag of clothes for donation that is sitting on the chair in the corner of my room!" What we don't want to happen is for all the Remove items to be piled up in your home somewhere for an eternity because now the actual decluttering is basically done, you have lost enthusiasm to completely finish the job.

If you are planning to throw everything in the trash, then you don't need to read this chapter. However, many of us want to declutter but worry about where all the stuff will end up. Avoiding decluttering because you think your things will add to landfills is not justifiable. You are transferring the decision-making burden about your stuff to future generations. And you are denying your items a life with someone else who will use or love them.

Yes, it will take more time and effort to sort through the Remove pile to divide it into donate, sell, or recycle. You will have questions. Where to give stuff to? What places want which things? What is the best way to sell an item? What can be recycled? And what the heck are upcycling and freecycling? All these questions will be answered in this chapter as it attempts to make taking action on your unwanted items as seamless as possible.

Note that you may sort out the Remove piles as you clear each area or at the end of the full home declutter. There is no one right way to attempt it.

Just get the stuff out of your house within a reasonable time period!

I couldn't imagine that other people would want my old things, but I have now flipped that belief around. From the friend who sent a photo of her toddler looking delighted in a pretty little dress I passed on, to the note of thanks I received from a domestic violence shelter after I donated a few unused toiletry items, to the person who paid over $100 for a desk that no one in my family wanted, knowing that others will happily receive your unwanted stuff makes taking action on it much less of a struggle.

Here are the main ways your Remove pile can be sorted:

- Trash
- Reuse
- Recycle
- Sell
- Give away

- Donate

This chapter discusses options in a general way. Please ask around or use the Internet to find the best approach to discard stuff in your local area.

TRASH

By all means put garbage in the trash. Things like dirty, worn clothes, broken, dangerous toys or bits of plastic packaging are usually fair contenders to go in the waste bin. Some items will be picked up by curbside garbage collectors, but others may require a trip to the nearest waste management transfer station.

Tossing something in the trash may seem like the easy option, but sometimes this isn't even the case. Batteries, paint, crockery and electrical cables are just some common declutter items that may not be accepted.

Stuff that is truly trash should be treated as such, but taking the time to identify the best destination for an item—although cumbersome—can alleviate pressure on your local landfill.

REUSE

Check your Remove pile for items you could reuse in your own home. Would you wear that blouse if you sewed that button back on? Would you play that old transistor radio if you replaced the batteries and reattached that loose wire? Would those old clothes cut up into rags be useful for washing your car, polishing shoes or dusting skirting boards? Could those old sheets be used for kids dress ups or as drop cloths for a painting job? Reusing gives items another life, even briefly, in your home, before truly becoming waste.

Whether something can be repaired is dependent on your skills in that area and how much time you wish to allocate to fixing it. But these days when you can watch a quick YouTube video that provides step-by-step instructions, a few minutes of industriousness may be worth your time and effort to make something useful again.

Upcycling transforms unwanted items into new or better-quality products. Upcycling is likely to take longer but the results are often unique and valuable. Baby bibs, girls' dresses or college t-shirts woven into a quilt, old curtains made into cushion covers or empty jars or bottles recrafted as lamps are all great upcycling ideas. Check out Etsy or Pinterest for more upcycling inspiration.

Yes, you may want to boot that thing out of the house, but check if you really won't use it in some form or another before it goes.

RECYCLE

Recycling is a method of converting waste materials into new objects. We know to recycle common household items such as glass, paper and plastic, but there are plenty of other items that can be recycled.

Electronic goods (sometimes known as e-waste) such as computers, mobile phones, TVs, stereos and printers, plus items such as batteries, light bulbs and old appliances can be dropped off at non-profit recycling organizations or government run centers, sometimes for free and sometimes for a fee.

Do a quick Internet search before getting rid of tricky items such as paint, tires, cables or scrap metal. Some special organizations do gratefully take and use these things.

Community workshops such as Men's Sheds (menzshed.org.nz) will fix up old bicycles, broken toys and appliances in need of quick repair and then donate them on. Of course, check first to see if they want the items you are offering. Not only does this help the environment, but these places provide a way for men and women to use their skills, teach others and help their local community—win-win.

SELL

Speaking of win-win—what can be better than having a tidy, spacious home? Getting cold hard cash for items that you no longer want! Make sure that what you are selling is in good condition or be honest if it needs repairing.

We have often had success putting '$1 reserve' items on TradeMe (the equivalent of eBay here) just to get them out of the house. Sometimes we make more than a few dollars from them.

You never know when your trash may be someone else's treasure.

Selling your things sounds amazing, but you need to know where you can sell, what can be sold and pitfalls to avoid so that selling your items is worth your time and effort.

You can sell online or offline via:

- Auction sites
- A garage or yard sale
- Markets, back of car sales or community tag sales
- Consignment stores or retailers
- Pawn shops or second-hand dealers
- Online websites known for selling things such as Craigslist or Facebook Marketplace

When people think of selling their things, often the first place that comes to mind is online auction sites such as eBay. For a fee taken out of your sales proceeds, you can list an item on their website and get buyers to bid on your unwanted goods. You decide whether you want payment in cash or via online banking and whether you want the buyer to pick it up, or if you prefer to mail it. You will need to set up an account, you may have to answer questions about the item, the fees can sometimes be higher than you would like and sometimes sales fall through, but it is often a convenient way of getting 'cash for your trash'.

Often only for expensive or rare items such as cars, jewelry or original art, offline auction companies may be the most appropriate place to sell something. They can take some time to investigate, there may be additional charges involved, and there is a chance your item won't sell for what you want or at all, but you may end up with more money via these professional organizations.

Garage or yard sales or selling at markets or via community ventures work best at the end of a declutter when you have everything you no longer want stored up and you attempt to sell it over the course of a morning or whole day. This can be fun but does involve advertising your wares in some form, pricing items, being available to hand them over and bartering with neighbors or strangers, often over a few cents.

Consignment stores are gaining in popularity. You hand over quality, pre-loved clothes, accessories, shoes, electronic items, books or other sought-after gear, and when the store sells it, you get paid out of the profits. All the upside without the hassle of trying to sell it yourself. Some consignment stores accept posted items and you don't even have to pay shipping! They may not want all your stuff, you may not get as much as you could for it, and some consignment stores have a time limit so that after, say,

12 months they won't pay out on an item. Even so, it is well worth researching local and online consignment stores and inquiring what items they will take.

I recently received an unexpected windfall of $43 from a maternity wear consignment store I had given clothes to over four years ago! It seems eerily coincidental that this bonus payout occurred while writing this book.

Pawn shops tend to have a bad name, but these days you can locate non-shady secondhand dealers that happily pay out on certain items. I had a few small pieces of gold jewelry that had little sentimental value and that I was never going to wear. I was thrilled to receive cash for them from the local secondhand dealer.

People have different degrees of success on other online selling platforms such as Craigslist and Facebook Marketplace. They are worth checking out, but as always, be vigilant about exchanging financial details online and giving out your address to strangers.

Give Away

Of course, you can simply give your things away. Sometimes this is the easiest way to jettison items. Donating items to charity will be discussed shortly, but know that giving away items isn't just for the needy.

You may have someone in mind to gift an item to, but don't offload onto unsuspecting family members or friends just because you can't be bothered to find the best way to discard an item. Ask and make sure they actually want it before handing it over.

Freecycling is the act of giving away usable items to others instead of them ending up in a landfill. Even if you have never heard of the word, you may have offered items for free on online auction sites like eBay or websites like Craigslist or announced on social media that you wish to give something away. Putting something up for free online means that someone, somewhere has a chance of using it even if you don't think it has any value.

One fun way to get rid of clothes, shoes, accessories, books and household items is to have a swap party. Tell your friends to bring their unwanted items to your home one evening, set up a temporary changing room, provide some wine and snacks and everyone goes home with something. It is like shopping without the exchange of cash. Any extra items that haven't found a home by the end of the evening can be donated.

DONATE

Due to the popularity of Marie Kondo and others, there are now headlines about charity stores and organizations being inundated with excess stuff. Please don't let that stop you from offering your unwanted items. If in doubt, pick up the phone and ask what they will take. Noticing that a couple of local charity stores had an embargo on accepting donated goods, I called another organization close by that was all too happy to accept the 14—yes 14!—bags of baby and toddler clothes I had stored up. I did tell them repeatedly that there were 14 bags.

Where you live will have numerous charitable and not-for-profit organizations that accept different types and varying quality of goods, so it is impossible to give specific advice. Look up or ask people in your area for recommendations. Here are some main ideas about where to send your unwanted items:

- Charity or thrift stores

- Non-profit organizations such as Salvation Army, Goodwill and Red Cross
- Homeless shelters
- Animal rescue and protection shelters
- Women's or domestic violence shelters
- Refugee organizations
- Hospitals, homes that care for the elderly and senior centers
- Churches and other religious organizations
- Libraries
- Schools
- Prisons

For good quality furniture, check which local non-profits offer free pick up—they are often the best way to get bulky items off your hands.

Clean, dry clothes are welcome at most places, sometimes even if they are stained, but check with them first. If you have good quality business attire, then 'Dress for Success', an organization that helps women re-enter the workforce, will take them. Don't think that ripped or worn clothes, linen and blankets are worthless. Textile recycling places and animal shelters are usually happy to receive such items.

Books can be welcome at libraries, schools, prisons, hospitals and aged care facilities. Check out if there is a 'Little Free Library' (littlefreelibrary.org) near you to give your books to and if there isn't, consider building one!

Sealed, unused toiletries and makeup that you don't need are wanted by some organizations, especially domestic violence and homeless shelters. Similarly, non-expired food items are usually welcomed in these places.

What about those one-offs and interesting items? You may not think that your old prescription glasses or your wedding dress would be wanted by anyone, but there are special organizations set up just to retrieve such things and allocate them out to people in need.

Lastly, if you have a physical copy of this very book that you do not think you will need to read again, consider selling, donating or giving it away. I would like to think that as many people as possible love or use it!

This chapter was written to get you excited to offload your unwanted goods. The next chapter will help you not to purchase them in the first place.

ACTION STEP

Get your Remove pile out of your house as soon as possible.

10
———

CHANGE

> 'Too many people spend money they haven't earned, to buy things they don't want, to impress people that they don't like.' – various attributions including Robert Quillen and Will Rogers

HOME INVASION

You can already see that having less has a positive impact on your kids—they don't fight as much, play with the toys they have and use their imaginations more. Your partner can now find things in the drawers and cupboards. And the extra space is making you feel calm, happy and in control of your life once again.

BUT... each and every day, more stuff is creeping back in, threatening to undo all your hard work. What do you do to stop the invasion of things?

First, appreciate that you have enough knowledge and motivation to never ever let your home get as cluttered as it was before. However, you must continue to be vigilant.

This chapter reminds you that your stuff doesn't really make you happy, helps you find out why you buy and provides suggestions to change your consumer behavior.

Consumption and Happiness

We are taught from a very young age that buying and owning things makes us happy. Just because it is 'normal' doesn't make it right. From the 5,000 advertising messages per day that consciously or subconsciously enter our minds, to the adoration of celebrities and billionaires and their glamorous lifestyles, we are programmed with the belief that more is better. It is ingrained in our modern culture—countries are doing well if their economies have high GDPs, even though that statistic is meaningless to most of us. Shopping is considered a pastime, a way to distract ourselves, something that is okay to do if we are bored.

The madness has got to stop. Right here. Right now.

You are in control of your beliefs and you can change them. You can decide that 'more' just complicates things and 'less' is what makes you happy. You can decide to put attention on things like creativity, quality time with your family and rest over being a cog-in-the-wheel consumer. You can decide to value saving money over that next impulse purchase.

You already know that clutter hasn't made you happy. Dare to join the growing movement that is trying to eradicate the connection between buying things and happiness.

You have everything you need right now to live a beautiful, amazing life.

As Erica Layne writes in *The Minimalist Way*: "we are using consumption to build lives that look good, let's limit our consumption and build lives that feel good."

WHY WE BUY

It is difficult to break free of consumer society. Giant shopping malls are constructed every week, the Internet has allowed 'add to cart' to happen 24/7 and algorithms now stalk what you search for and present ads for your latest desires that are only one click away. Everything is set up so you buy more—stores have set layouts that you unconsciously memorize, they offer loyalty cards and in-store credit cards, they present 'too good to be true' bargain basement sales and give you samples or gifts with purchase.

It is not your fault but it IS your responsibility.

Why you buy will be different between people and also depends on what you are buying. Understanding the three main reasons why you buy—and why they don't serve you—will stop unnecessary consumption and keep your hard-earned money in your back pocket.

- **We buy to feel good** – Instead of coaching or counseling, we indulge in 'retail therapy'. We may get an initial hit of joy but it dissipates fast. Despite all the messages that this thing or that thing will make us happier, more successful, prettier, a better mama or an incredible human, the pleasure we seek never lasts.

Then what do we do? Jump back on the hedonistic treadmill and try to satisfy ourselves all over again.

- **We buy to convey status** – We want the latest car / phone / shoes to keep up with the Joneses. But the Joneses don't exist! We compare ourselves to others and find ourselves lacking due to cultural messages and slick marketing, not because of any real need. If you have a roof over your head and food on the table, you are more fortunate than millions of people, so don't succumb to this nonsensical pressure to buy, accumulate and conform.

- **We buy to avoid missing out** – Our brains put us on red alert any time we perceive there is scarcity because in prehistoric times, lack (of water, food, shelter) could mean misery or death. We now live in abundant times and scarcity is contrived by retailers to encourage us to buy now. Phrases such as 'bargain', 'clearance sale', 'today only' and 'just 5 left' are ways to convey scarcity when there really is none. Don't worry if you 'miss out', there will always be another sale, and if there isn't, you are now well on your way to being content with what you already have.

Now that you know your clutter doesn't make you truly happy and the reasons you buy are nothing but mirages, what are some practical ways you can thwart, or at least significantly diminish, the influx?

Don't Tempt Yourself

Get on the offensive and reduce your temptation to buy. Stop the marketing barrage by watching less TV that glamorizes certain lifestyles and interrupts them with commercials that tell you that you aren't enough unless you get this new thing now. Have breaks from scrolling through social media, which basically does the same thing, albeit with sophisticated algorithms that know exactly what you want and present it to you frequently in the most appealing ways possible. Unsubscribe from daily deal sites, delete retailer newsletters, cut up store credit cards and request that no junk mail is sent to you. And never watch the shopping channel, ever!

Don't shop for fun. Find another recreational pursuit. Don't enter a store or even window shop if it is too tempting. If you go out, experiment with leaving your wallet at home.

If you must go to the store, bring a list and stick to it, not just for the supermarket but for any shopping you do. Some people bring only the cash they need or a caring friend who stops them from purchasing impulsively.

DON'T ACCEPT FREEBIES

Here is a quick way to not fill up your house with things you don't really need—say 'no' to freebies and giveaways. Don't fill your suitcase with shampoos and soaps from your hotel room. Don't take that sample, trial size, magnet, pen, free toaster or gift with purchase. This can take practice as it feels ungrateful to say 'no' to free stuff, but why not try it? It is unlikely that you will regret NOT taking that drink bottle or the collector cards next time your local supermarket is having a promotion. More on how to say 'no' in the next chapter.

DON'T BUY

Here is the simplest suggestion. Simple but not easy: don't buy anything. Don't purchase at the store. Don't add to cart online. I can already hear the "but, but, but". Of course, on a day-to-day basis, you can still shop for fresh food items, buy household necessities you have completely run out of or pick up urgent needs like medicines.

Many families attempt this as a kind of a fun experiment for a period of time. They challenge themselves to not buy anything for a week / one month / three months / a whole year. They find themselves getting resourceful and using something else in its place, making do without or asking others if they need something (more on borrowing below). This may mean a ban on buying all non-essential household items or a prohibition on purchasing one category of things, for example, clothes.

Another idea is stop buying items you habitually consume and see if you really want or use them. Could you go without cable? Does everyone in the household need a different type of conditioner? Would anyone mind if you didn't decorate your house up to the hilt for Halloween or Christmas? Do you really need to replace that broken food processor? Just because you have always done it like that or had one of those doesn't mean you have to continue in the same way.

Others have policies in place to stop relentless consumption. I now very rarely buy greeting cards and instead ask the kids to make them. On vacation, we try not to buy souvenirs, reminding the kids that photos and memories of our fun adventures together are enough. You can grow, produce or make your own to reduce the need for buying. We enjoy picking from our summer vegetable garden and others we know make their own bread or soaps or keep chickens for eggs.

BUY CONSCIOUSLY

Decluttering your home is not some sort of panacea that miraculously stops you from wanting things. You will still covet pretty things. Maybe not so much as before, but the desire will remain. However, purchasing in a more conscious manner means you won't buy as much. Before you buy something, give yourself time for an honest consideration of whether you truly need to own it.

One way to do this is to pause. Give yourself some breathing room between the wanting and the buying of something. Delayed gratification can be a good thing. For large appliances or expensive items like cars, waiting 30 days before purchasing is a good rule of thumb. Technology like computers and TVs usually have an even better product on offer 30 days from now. Give yourself 24 hours between 'add to cart' and purchase. That cute top, latest gadget or joke gift item that you clicked on in the wee hours may not seem so appealing in the light of day.

You can ask questions before you buy. Grill yourself like you are in court and you need to defend your buying decision. Do I need it at all? Do I need it now? Do I need to buy it brand new? How much will I really use it? Will this thing last a long time? Is it easy to take care of? Does this have a place in my home? Can it really make my life easier or does it just add complication? Would I prefer to spend money on something else that I would enjoy more?

This minimalism journey peels back the layers and allows you to be who you truly are. This is amazing in its own right but as an added bonus it also helps you buy only things that you actually love and use. You don't have to follow fads—you can have your own style and not buy the latest fashion. Worrying about what others think is eliminated so you don't need to buy to keep up with the imaginary Joneses. And you don't have to live a fantasy life that includes purchasing things for hobbies you are never going to pursue.

You get to buy for you, the real you.

BUY QUALITY

I am currently wearing a pair of Ugg boots (sturdy boot-like slippers) that seemed expensive at the time. I was shocked when my boyfriend admitted how much he had spent on them. Well, that was over 20 years ago and that particular boyfriend is long gone, but I have worn the $80 pair of Ugg boots almost every day since and they are still going strong.

Buying quality sounds elitist but it is simply asking you to invest in the best you can afford. It doesn't apply to everything: my kids either ruin, lose or grow out of their shoes so fast that the additional expense is hardly worth it. This principle is asking you not to buy JUST because something is cheap or on sale. You don't have to partake in our throwaway culture because everyone else seems to.

What connotes quality? Look for locally or ethically made, natural materials or ingredients plus items that are sustainably produced or not excessively packaged. Not sure where it came from or what is made out of? Start being curious. Ask.

There are many benefits, like less waste for you and the planet, saving money in the long run as it lasts longer so you do not have to replace it as often, plus you show your kids how important it is to look after and be responsible for your vital few possessions.

BUY SECONDHAND

Although it seems like conflicting advice to buying quality, buying secondhand is also a viable option. In fact, some secondhand items, built or made when things were created to last, are often better quality than their newer versions—think of your parents' electric mixer or lawnmower that just kept going. Purchasing secondhand helps your wallet, is better for the environment plus purchasing from charity stores helps support non-profit organizations, a complete win-win.

RENT, HIRE, BORROW

One of the first questions to ask yourself whenever you want to buy something is, do I really need to own this? Would it suit my needs better to hire or borrow it?

Depending on who you talk to, 'rent' and 'hire' can have slightly different meanings, but here they both mean paying money for the use of something for a limited period. Borrowing implies that you get the use of the thing for free. If you are not sure where to hire or borrow from, ask friends, enquire locally or search online.

Renting and borrowing products and services is now extremely trendy. Millennials, especially, don't want to own things, they just want access to them. Many people now choose to rent an Airbnb, get a rideshare like Uber or use a subscription model for their entertainment needs—think Spotify for music and Netflix for TV. This sharing economy is not only environmentally and economically sustainable, it is very cool.

You are probably already participating—for instance, by borrowing books from the library or swapping fruit and vegetables you grow with your neighbors. Decide to expand your net even wider.

What sort of things are good contenders to be hired or borrowed?

- Equipment or items for one-off events, e.g.: extra chairs or glasses for a party or a dress to wear to a wedding
- Expensive items you are not sure you want to buy e.g.: kids' sports equipment, music instruments or a workshop tool
- Things your children will grow out of quickly e.g.: baby gear or toys

Think of the benefits: you save money, it is a better use of resources and you don't have it filling up your space indefinitely. Plus, if you do decide to purchase it, you get to try before you buy, so you know it works for you. In addition, it encourages more social interaction and sharing within your community.

GIFTS

When I was younger, I worked part-time in a department store and spent every festive season for five years in the cosmetics section. Men would rush in on Christmas Eve and frantically wave cash at me while pointing to the nearest gift-wrapped perfume set. They didn't want to smell the fragrance, they just wanted something they could grab quickly and toss under the tree for their wives. How is that in the spirit of Christmas?

You can take charge of buying or not buying things for yourself, but what do you do about gifts? In the scheme of things, most people don't race into a store and throw cash at an assistant to grab whatever is available. Someone who cares for you has taken the time, money and effort to think of getting something, wrapping it and lovingly presenting it to you or your kids. As giving and receiving gifts is one of the Five Love Languages, it is important to tread carefully on the fine line between not wanting to add clutter to your home and trying not to offend.

The fairest thing to do is to set up rules and guidelines for gifts. You can change family traditions and revise expectations with your friends. These may get some push back, but if they are clearly and gracefully communicated, then how others respond is not your problem. Choose an idea that you think would work or test out a recommendation and see if it goes smoothly.

Here are some suggestions for limiting traditional gift-giving:

- Don't buy toys as a reward for good behavior or achievement, simply praise or find alternative ways to celebrate
- Understand that just because it is Valentine's Day, Mother's Day, Father's Day or even Christmas, it does NOT mean that gift giving has to be involved
- Make birthdays and special days about family time, fun activities with friends or lunches or dinners out at cafes or restaurants instead of an actual gift
- Have agreements with your close friends that you will exchange gifts on birthdays but not on other occasions like Christmas (for them and their kids)
- Pool together to buy one big gift rather than lots of small, cheaper gifts, e.g.: a few friends buy one large LEGO set or family members pitch in to buy a bike
- Limit the number of gifts each family member expects to receive, for instance, in our family, there is only one gift given to each adult at Christmas
- Include a gift exchange card if it is possible to do so
- Ask for experiences rather than things—more ideas below

Here are some experience ideas as an alternative to 'thing' gifts. You can always wrap the voucher up or put a bow on it to make the presentation beautiful. You can, say, provide three ideas and get the gift giver to choose one so you experience an element of surprise. Most of these ideas are applicable to both grown-ups and children:

- Facial or massage vouchers (for adults)
- Tickets to movies, concerts and other events
- Going out for ice-cream, bowling or mini-golf
- Classes or memberships, e.g.: an art class, one-year zoo pass
- A trial for a fun or challenging activity, e.g.: rock climbing or archery
- Donation to your favorite charity

One fantastic experience gift idea is to get any teenager or adult in your life a personal styling experience. This is a fun hour or two for the recipient and in the long run, it saves a lot of time and money on not trying on and buying the wrong clothes, accessories and makeup.

Homemade and creative gifts make a special present for loved ones. You can:

- Bake cookies or cupcakes or make breakfast in bed
- Write them a special note, play a song or draw them a picture
- Create a coupon for unlimited hugs, to do the washing up for a week or to babysit for an evening

If people in your life insist on getting your kids a gift and want to get them someTHING, then the classics are usually your best options, i.e.:

- Books
- Art and craft materials

- Blocks (wooden blocks, LEGO)
- Cars, trains and other transportation-related toys
- Board games that the whole family can enjoy playing
- Outside play equipment like a football or a basketball hoop

Kids birthday parties are especially tricky to navigate when it comes to gifts. One way to stop this problem is to not have a birthday party. This sounds mean, but for kids under three, this is usually no problem, and for kids older than eight, you can have a small group do a fun activity together or have a sleepover instead of an actual party.

Any attempt to reduce the number of gifts at your child's birthday party can be met with resistance from your youngster or annoyance from parents of kids that are invited. You can announce on the invites that you have a preference for no gifts at all or request a small donation to charity or ask for a contribution of a few dollars to the birthday party expenses like the entertainment or a bouncy castle in lieu of a gift. How people respond to these options varies from "what a great idea" to being outed as presumptuous, mean-spirited or rude. Give it a go if you like, but be aware of the potential pitfalls.

Even if you have clearly stated you don't want a gift or only want a certain type of gift, if someone presents you with a wrapped present for you or your kids, warmly accept it and say a big thank you. What you decide to do with that gift—re-gift it, donate it or return it to the store and exchange it for something else—has nothing to do with the giver. Sometimes, though, the person may have given you something you didn't even know you wanted that is perfect for you. Let yourself receive gifts with pleasure and grace when they are offered.

. . .

THRIVE NOT DIVE

Remember that minimalism means you can still buy things! The economy is not going to take a dive because you alter your consumer behavior to now only accept quality goods you love and cherish. Civilization is not going to tank if your seven-year-old doesn't receive his weight in plastic toys. In fact, paying for quality goods, fun activities or family experiences will help many businesses thrive.

Changing your consumer behavior is one step in the journey to embracing a minimalist lifestyle. The next chapter gives suggestions for how you can continue down the 'less is more' path.

ACTION STEP

As a fun challenge, don't buy anything for a week. Let me know how it goes.

11

EMBRACE

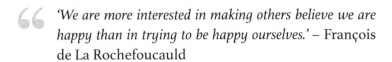 *'We are more interested in making others believe we are happy than in trying to be happy ourselves.'* – François de La Rochefoucauld

MINIMALISM 1.0

At the start of the book, minimalism was described as a tool to help you curate and focus on the essentials and use what is important in your life to create more of what you crave: security, joy, meaning and freedom.

What is so great about this definition is that you can apply it in the best way for you and your family. There is no one right way to 'do' minimalism. Now that you know the advantages of decluttering your belongings, you will start to wonder what else can be decluttered to make way for what you really want in life.

This chapter offers three minimalist suggestions that are hugely beneficial to you and your family. It doesn't list everything you could embrace, but it gives you a taste of what decluttering your life—and not just your home—can look and feel like.

CONTENTMENT AND GRATITUDE

Within the minimalism movement there is a focus on enjoying what you have. This should be easy because what you now keep around, you love or use. Contentment can emerge in a number of ways: not comparing yourself to others, enjoying the present moment or being generous with your time and money.

One simple way to promote this contentment mindset is to develop a daily gratitude practice. Find a practice that you can stick to and do it every day. It is the everyday nature of gratitude that is important, not what you do, how long it takes or even what your responses are.

Do this exercise on your own, with your partner or with the kids, on the way to school or work, over breakfast or dinner, or at bedtime.

Ask the following two questions:

- What are you grateful for?
- What are you happy about?

I often say something more profound, life affirming or esoteric for my grateful answer (the sun, clean running water, good health). Then I respond with something more ridiculous or materialistic or frivolous for the happy one (my favorite TV program, chocolate or a new podcast I have discovered). You can list many things or settle on one.

There are other appreciation practices you can adopt instead of, or as well as, the one above. Select one or two that resonate with you and make them into a habit:

- Start a gratitude list and share it via email with a few friends
- Write three things you are grateful for each day in a journal
- Put a sheet of paper on the fridge to which everyone in the family can add a gratitude item
- Once a week, at dinnertime, speak your appreciation to others at the table
- Create a 'Gratitude Photo Album' of images you love and keep it private or share it on social media
- If you can't get to sleep, do an alphabet appreciation exercise: think of something you are grateful for starting with A then B, and onward—believe me, you won't make it to Z

Overall, contentment and gratitude are about deciding to be happy no matter what.

Boundaries and Saying No

Embracing minimalism means putting up some firm boundaries so you let in only what is important and keep out the rest. Creating boundaries comes in many forms: not putting your work email on your phone, reducing your kids' activities to one per week or routinely being in bed before 10pm.

Putting in boundaries will be difficult, at least at first. To apply this in a real-world setting, you need to practice saying 'no'.

If you do not learn to say 'no', then you are saying 'yes' to someone else's agenda and 'no' to yourself. You are saying 'yes' to that school committee meeting and 'no' to watching your kid's football game. You are saying 'yes' to organizing that workshop for your boss after hours and 'no' to going to that yoga class. You are saying 'yes' to tidying up toys when your children are asleep and 'no' to going to bed at a reasonable time.

You can be a lovely person and say 'no'. Author, researcher and TED speaker, Brené Brown, says, "Compassionate people ask for what they need. They say no when they need to, and when they say yes, they mean it. They're compassionate because their boundaries keep them out of resentment."

Even in the nicest way possible, saying 'no' is uncomfortable, so practice on small things and build up. Here are a few ways to say 'no' politely:

- "Sounds wonderful, but that is not part of my work focus right now."
- "Sorry but my current commitments mean I cannot take that on."
- "It sounds amazing but I wouldn't be able to give that the attention it deserves."
- "I can't help you right now but I can schedule it after X date."
- "Sorry it is not my policy to do X." (People respect policies, even ones you have made up yourself!)

If a 'no' is done well, people should be happy with how clear you are and how committed you are to what is important to you. And if they are not happy? Well, their response is their problem.

TAKING CARE OF YOURSELF AND CUTTING DIGITAL DISTRACTIONS

We rush from one thing to another, barely pausing for a breath. Sitting down to eat lunch, getting eight hours of solid sleep each night and basking in the warm sun for a few minutes per day are now unheard-of luxuries.

Yet self-care in all its forms, especially play and rest, is the backbone to a beautiful life.

Busyness can't be fully eliminated from your life, but you can make headway to reduce feeling so frantic and overwhelmed. You take care of your precious, few, remaining things so you can learn to take care of yourself, too. One practical way to do this is to be more screen free.

Did you know that we typically spend over three hours per day on our smart phones? Or that, on average, a phone is picked up an incredible 50 times per day? Or that—and this is embarrassing —70% of us look at another device while watching TV?

It was hard enough a few years back to stay focused, but now, as Jen Sincero says in *You are a Badass*, we are so distracted it is a wonder we still speak in full sentences.

Ways to reduce digital distractions:

Turn off your push notifications. Please people! You don't need the latest celebrity tweet or WhatsApp group message flickering onto your smart phone screen every four seconds. Keep your important calendar reminders on but turn the rest of them off! I am not going to tell you exactly how to do it as it is different for each device. Start by going into your settings for the relevant apps and switch any push notifications to OFF. Please. Now.

Do a digital declutter. Don't know where to start? Here are some ideas: unsubscribe from emails you don't need (especially those daily deal ones), delete emails that you have taken action on, put other emails in folders, remove apps you don't use and unfollow social media pages, groups and people that you don't want to see in your feed anymore.

Change your habits with your smart phone or device. Things I try to do:

- No second screen in the room while watching a TV program or movie.
- Look at social media no more than three times per day plus have a social media free Sunday.
- Do not give my phone a quick glance any time I am waiting or could be bored, like when I am standing in line, waiting for the kids to finish something or, er, at the traffic lights. If it's a short wait I challenge myself to look around. Yes, at the world. Notice things. If it's a long wait, I always have an interesting article saved or a book to read on my Kindle or Apple Books apps on my phone.
- Bonus tip: wear a watch. When I wear a watch I am not pulling my phone out to look at the time and then swiping to check something.

Yes, these are difficult at first but looking at your phone is merely a habit, one that keeps you staying busy. Stopping to allow space for some essential self-care is frightening—what if the world collapses while you are at Pilates class?—but once you make it a non-negotiable and feel its benefits, you won't want to return to your rushing ways.

Minimalism 2.0

This chapter only discusses three applications of minimalism. There are plenty of others. You can regain a focus on finances by using budgeting, having purchase restrictions and doing weekly meal planning. Others put routines in place so that they can prioritize family dinner time and leisurely weekends. Some use this new outlook to review their friendships and let go of ones that are no longer serving them. Many expand it out to decluttering negative thoughts by talking to a therapist or practicing meditation or affirmations. Some embrace the extra room in their lives to allow themselves to be idle—dream, wander, be curious and see where it takes them.

A minimalist approach teaches us that we don't have to live like anyone else.

We get to choose to direct our attention to what we value the most and include only the most vital in our day-to-day lives.

The final chapter wraps everything up with a brief discussion about the paradoxes highlighted by minimalism.

ACTION STEP

Embrace minimalism in at least one additional way: start a gratitude practice, say 'no' or challenge yourself to a digital detox today.

12

THE PARADOXES OF MINIMALISM

> 'Happiness resides not in possessions, and not in gold, happiness dwells in the soul.' – Democritus

ABSURDLY SIMPLE

Minimalism as an ideology is absurdly simple. It is a focus on what is essential for you. The reason it's difficult to fully embrace a minimalist outlook is that it throws up a number of paradoxes. Let's examine them.

PARADOX ONE: WE LIVE MORE WHEN WE OWN LESS

Only by unshackling ourselves from the things that we think make us who we are can we become who we are meant to be. As Arianna Huffington says in *Thrive*: "we are not on this earth to accumulate victories or trophies but to be whittled down until what is left is who we truly are."

. . .

Paradox Two: To Live a Bigger Life Requires a Focus on the Most Ordinary

Living life well is within your grasp. Appreciate your gorgeous children. Develop deep connections with loved ones. Read a good book now and then. Heartfully participate in your community. Get on with what really matters despite how mundane it may seem.

Paradox Three: Security Arises from Letting Go

By rigidly holding onto your stuff, it actually controls you. Letting go of consuming and conforming means that you gain back control of your life. Investing in a life you can be proud of seems riskier but provides a certainty of having no regrets.

Space Paradox

These contradictory statements may be hard to wrap your head around, but don't let that put you off embracing a minimalist approach to life. After all, the reality we are all currently living in has its own paradoxes that we conveniently ignore.

An especially prevalent one is to express the need for more room to breathe while staying as busy as possible. We say we want more space, yet we fill up our lives with unnecessary stuff, crowded schedules and mindless distractions.

I get it! Space is scary as it means you no longer have any excuse not to focus on what is important. You cannot hide. But saying you want space while clicking 'add to cart' is a paradox that I, for one, am no longer content to put up with.

Space may be frightening but it is the only way to shine.

The Minimalism Paradox

Marie Kondo writes that putting your house in order allows your life to truly begin. Many people think they need to declutter their homes to declutter their lives, that transforming their external space is a gateway to shift internally as well, that they need to DO something in order to BE who they want to be.

Minimalism directs you from decluttering your home to decluttering your life. But it doesn't need to be this way. It is not, as we are led to believe, a necessary first step.

Decluttering your home can jumpstart a minimalist mindset, but you can switch on the motor at any time. Your engine is in perfect working order, you just need turn the key.

Whether or not you keep your wedding dress / treadmill / popcorn machine is not the issue. Regardless of what you decide in your decluttering efforts, you can give yourself permission to have more energy, more quality time with your family, more money and more opportunity to pursue your dreams.

You don't need space in your home for that, you need space in your mind, heart and soul.

No Paradox

Minimalism is ultimately about trying to create more security, joy, meaning and freedom for what is most important.

Security doesn't come from the stuff you own, but from living a life of no regrets. Instead of joy being found in your things, you can now find it in enhancing your close relationships and growing through new experiences. As an alternative to finding meaning in consuming more, you can now pursue more a purposeful life that centers around creativity, connection and contribution. And not being able to distract yourself with your stuff enables you to tap into the freedom to dream big and step into your generous heart.

In the end there is no paradox.

When you pass away, you will be remembered for your beliefs, your passions, the lives you touched and how you grew as a human rather than for anything you owned.

Don't wait another second to spend your life building the relationships, creating the experiences and being grateful for the vital few possessions that you absolutely cherish.

APPENDIX

SIMPLIFY GAME PLAN

Here is the Simplify Game Plan you can adapt to suit you:

- Do a walk-through of your house with fresh eyes
- Schedule a time you can dedicate to decluttering, with others or on your own
- Choose a room or category or part of an area or category to declutter
- Optional – take a 'before' photo of the space as it is
- Pull everything out of the space that you are decluttering
- Optional – give the area a clean when everything is out of it
- Look at or pick up each item and decide between Remain, Remove, Relocate or Really Don't Know and put in assigned piles, bags or boxes
- An item should remain if you love it or use it
- Place all the Remain items back into the space they came from in a tidy way and as they best fit
- Optional – take an 'after' photo of the space as it is now

- Say thank you and goodbye to the items you put in the Remove pile if that floats your boat
- Give yourself permission to celebrate and include mini-rewards in the process
- Rinse and repeat until decluttering is finished
- Take the Relocate items to the where you think they should be in your home and place them there for now
- Sort the Remove pile at the end of decluttering into trash, reuse, recycle, sell, give away or donate and action accordingly
- Address the Really Don't Know pile—either assign it another classification or put it away for a few months and then review it again

READER GIFT: THE HAPPY20

There is no doubt that decluttering improves your life, but you can choose to be happy any time.
To remind you to squeeze the best out every single day, I created:

THE HAPPY20
20 Free Ways to Boost Happiness in 20 Seconds or Less

A PDF gift for you with quick ideas to improve your mood and add a little sparkle to your day.

Head to **JulieSchooler.com/gift** to grab your copy today.

ABOUT THE AUTHOR

Julie had aspirations of being a writer since she was very young but somehow got sidetracked into the corporate world. After the birth of her first child, she rediscovered her creative side. You can find her at JulieSchooler.com.

Her *Easy Peasy* books provide simple and straightforward information on parenting topics. The *Nourish Your Soul* series shares delicious wisdom to feel calmer, happier and more fulfilled.

Busy people can avoid wasting time searching for often confusing and conflicting advice and instead spend time with the beautiful tiny humans in their lives and do what makes their hearts sing.

Julie lives with her family in a small, magnificent country at the bottom of the world where you may find her trying to bake the perfect chocolate brownie.

BOOKS BY JULIE SCHOOLER

Easy Peasy **Books**

Easy Peasy Potty Training

Easy Peasy Healthy Eating

Nourish Your Soul **Books**

Rediscover Your Sparkle

Crappy to Happy

Embrace Your Awesomeness

Bucket List Blueprint

Super Sexy Goal Setting

Find Your Purpose in 15 Minutes

Clutter-Free Forever

Children's Picture Books

Maxy-Moo Flies to the Moon

Collections

Change Your Life 3-in-1 Collection

Rebelliously Happy 3-in-1 Collection

JulieSchooler.com/books

ACKNOWLEDGMENTS

This book would not have happened without Chrissy, who told me she was waiting for me to write it so she could use it to declutter her home. Here it is, busy mama!

Thank you, Sarah C, for lending me your books on decluttering. Apologies that I kept them for so long. I owe you late fees.

To Andrew and our two beautiful tiny humans, Dylan and Eloise. I live in a perpetual state of astonishment about how fortunate my life is. Thank you for making me laugh every single day.

PLEASE LEAVE A REVIEW

Clutter-Free Forever

Embrace Minimalism, Declutter Your Life and Never Iron Again

THANK YOU FOR READING THIS BOOK

I devoted many months to researching and writing this book. I then spent more time having it professionally edited, working with a designer to create an awesome cover and launching it into the world.

Time, money and heart has gone into this book and I very much hope you enjoyed reading it as much as I loved creating it.

It would mean the world to me if you could spend a few minutes writing a review on Goodreads or the online store where you purchased this book.

A review can be as short or long as you like and should be helpful and honest to assist other potential buyers of the book.

Reviews provide social proof that people like and recommend the book. More book reviews mean more book sales which means I can write more books.

Your book review helps me, as an independent author, more than you could ever know. I read every single review and when I get five-star review it absolutely makes my day.

Thanks, Julie.

REFERENCES

Resources

This book is a result of extensive research about decluttering and minimalism using articles, blog posts, podcasts, documentaries and TEDx talks, plus websites such as:

The Minimalists

Becoming Minimalist

The Life on Purpose Movement

Prosperity Kitchen

The Great Eco Journey

Books

Authentic Happiness – Using the New Positive Psychology to Realize Your Potential for Lasting Fulfillment – Martin Seligman, Ph.D. (US, 2002)

Clutterfree with Kids – Change Your Thinking, Discover New Habits, Free Your Home – Joshua Becker (US, 2014)

Cut the Clutter – A Simple Organization Plan for a Clean and Tidy Home – Cynthia Townley Ewer (US, 2016)

Declutter – The Get-Real Guide to Creating Calm from Chaos – Debora Robertson (UK, 2018)

Declutter Your Life – How Outer Order Leads to Inner Calm – Gill Hasson (UK, 2018)

Decluttering at the Speed of Life – Winning Your Never-Ending Battle with Stuff – Dana K. White (US, 2018)

Do Less – A Minimalist Guide to a Simplified, Organized, and Happy Life – Rachel Jonat (US, 2014)

Do Less – A Revolutionary Approach to Time and Energy Management for Busy Moms – Kate Northrup (US, 2019)

Easy Minimalist Living – 30 Days to Declutter, Simplify and Organize Your Home Without Driving Everyone Crazy – Jennifer Nicole (US, 2015)

Essentialism – The Disciplined Pursuit of Less – Greg McKeown (US, 2014)

Goodbye, Things – On Minimalist Living – Fumio Sasaki (UK, 2017)

Lillian Too's 168 Ways to Declutter Your Home and Re-energize Your Life – Lillian Too (US, 2016)

References

Minimalism – Live a Meaningful Life – Joshua Fields Millburn and Ryan Nicodemus (US, 2016)

Minimalism for Families – Practical Minimalist Living Strategies to Simplify Your Home and Life – Zoe Kim (US, 2017)

Spark Joy – An Illustrated Master Class on the Art of Organizing and Tidying Up – Marie Kondo (US, 2016)

Start with Your Sock Drawer and the Rest Will Follow – The Simple Guide to Living a Less Cluttered Life – Vicky Silverthorn with Emma Cooling (UK, 2016)

Steering by Starlight – The Science and Magic of Finding Your Destiny – Martha Beck (US, 2008)

The Busy Woman's Guide to High Energy Happiness – Louise Thompson (NZ, 2014)

The Happiness Project – Gretchen Rubin (USA, 2009)

The Five Love Languages – The Secret to Love That Lasts – Gary Chapman (US, 1992)

The Joy of Less – A Minimalist Guide to Declutter, Organize, and Simplify – Francine Jay (US, 2010)

The Life-Changing Magic of Tidying Up – The Japanese Art of Decluttering and Organizing – Marie Kondo (US, 2014)

The Minimalist Way – Minimalist Strategies to Declutter Your Life and Make Room for Joy – Erica Layne (US, 2019)

The More of Less – Finding the Life You Want Under Everything You Own – Joshua Becker (US, 2016)

*The Subtle Art of Not Giving a F*ck – A Counterintuitive Approach to Living a Good Life* – Mark Manson (US, 2016)

The Top Five Regrets of the Dying – A Life Transformed by the Dearly Departed – Bronnie Ware (US, 2011)

The Winner's Bible – Rewire Your Brain for Permanent Change – Dr. Kerry Spackman (USA, 2009)

Thrive – The Third Metric to Redefining Success and Creating a Life of Wellbeing, Wisdom and Wonder – Arianna Huffington (US, 2014)

Unstuffed – Decluttering Your Home, Mind and Soul – Ruth Soukup (US, 2016)

You are a Badass – How to Stop Doubting Your Greatness and Start Living an Awesome Life – Jen Sincero (US, 2013)

Printed in Great Britain
by Amazon